The Oasthouses

Their Life and Times

by

Alan Major

S. B. Publications

First published in 2006 by S. B. Publications
Tel: 01323 893498
Email: sbpublications@tiscali.co.uk
www.sbpublications.co.uk

ISBN 1-85770-319-7

Designed and Typeset by EH Graphics (01273) 515527

The Oasthouses - Their Life and Times

'O people, they come from far and wide
With a Morris car and a shilling guide
And a man may reckon his time well spent
Counting the castle walls of Kent.
Dover, Rochester, so he reads,
Tonbridge, Allington, Upnor, Leeds,
These are the scenes of doughty deeds
And when he is looking round for these
He notices, among the trees,
Curious towers with conical tops,
They're hundreds strong in the land.
"What are they?" Surely a child can tell.
"These are the castles of Kent as well".'

Thus wrote Donald Maxwell, Kent author-artist, in his The Enchanted Road, page 138, published Methuen, 1927. The 'curious towers with conical tops', as every Kent-born person will know, are a feature of the familiar oasts or oasthouses.

About the Author

Alan Major was born in Gillingham, 1929, but grew up at nearby Rainham, where he lived intil 1969. After education at Rainham's Council School and Senior School and training at Medway College of Arts and Crafts, Rochester, he worked as a printing trade typesetter in Rainham and Chatham. From 1950 to 1965 he wrote articles in his spare time until the latter years when he decided to attempt his childhood ambition 'to be an author' full-time, as he still is. His early books concerned natural history subjects but later books covered various aspects of the county of his birth.

Other books on Kent by the same author:

A New Dictionary of Kent Dialect.	Meresborough Books.
Who's Buried Where in Kent.	Meresborough Books.
Hidden Kent.	Countryside Books.
Cherries in the Rise.	S.B. Publications.
Goldings, Napoleons and Romneys.	S.B. Publications.
A Kentish Childhood.	S.B. Publications.
Kentish As She Wus Spoke.	S.B. Publications.
A Little Book of Kent.	S.B. Publications.
The Neat and Nippy Guide to Canterbury.	S.B. Publications.
The Kentish Lights.	S.B. Publications.
A Kent Quiz Book.	S.B. Publications.

Contents

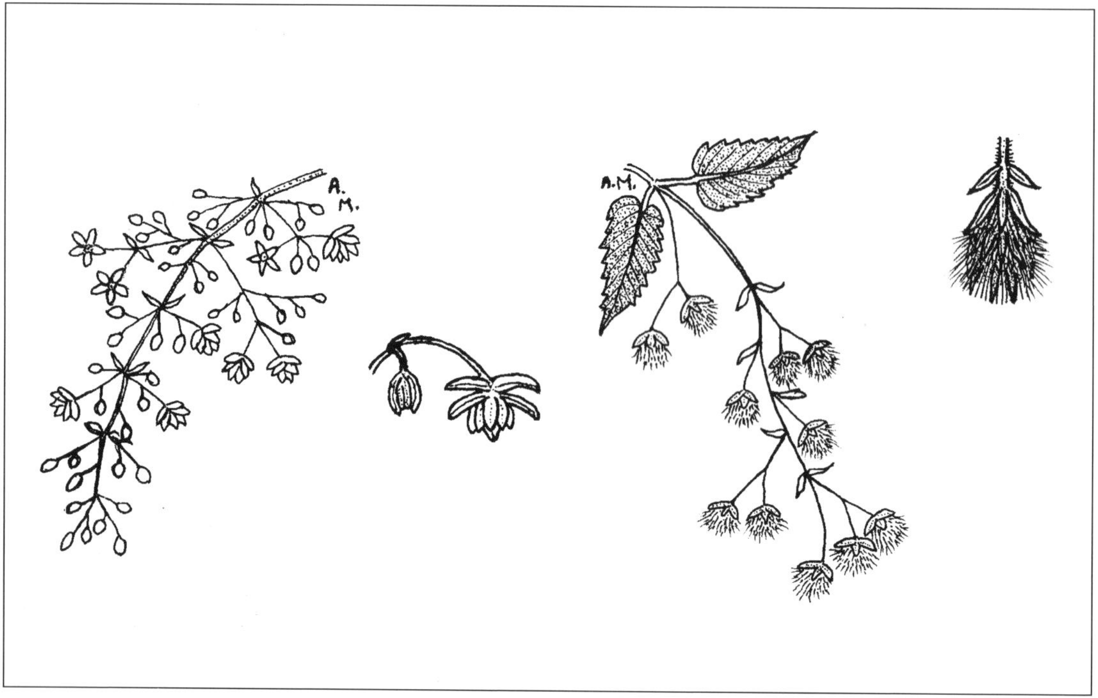

Male hop flower (enlarged).

Female hop flower (enlarged).

What's In A Name?

An oast is, or was if no longer in intended use, the building where freshly picked green hops were received to be dried, cooled, pocketed, prior to despatch to brewers or hop merchants.

The growing of hops, the people who grew them and those who picked them have almost vanished into the history and folklore of Kent and Sussex, but the oasts/oasthouses survive in former hop cultivation districts of these counties, reminders of now-gone 'hopping' days.

Oast and oasthouse seem curious words to be in the vocabulary of these counties. According to the Oxford English Dictionary oast was derived from the Old Latin aestus - heat, and aidis - hearth or house. Variations - host, ast, nost - were used in the 15th century for a building wherein were dried lime and bricks, or malt was prepared. The words est, eest, east, meaning 'a drying kiln', were introduced into Kent in the 16th century, used by the Flemish hop growers and merchants from Flanders where commercial hop growing was successfully longtime established. Other variations - oste, oost, oust, ost - with the same meaning, were also used in the following two centuries. In time these words were corrupted with use in the Kentish speech pronunciation to oast. By the 19th century oast referred only to 'a place where hops are or were dried'. Oasthouse first appeared in use in the 18th century, pronounced as westus or wo-stus in Kent dialect. The shorter term oast was and is most often used by hop growers and oasthouse by the rural and urban general public.

And A Hop Is?

To understand the need for oasthouses it is necessary to explain the Hop, the circumstances of its origin and cultivation.

The Hop can be seen in hedgerows in Kent, Sussex and elsewhere in southern England. Hop bines (plants) in these habitats may be the truly native Wild Hop but are sometimes indicative there had been a hop garden thereabouts in the past which was 'grubbed up', the land used for another purpose later, but roots of hop bines were deliberately discarded or 'escaped' into the hedgebottom and became established. Aptly, by the way, in 2004 the Hop was chosen as the county flower symbol of Kent.

In early April several long, tough, rough to the touch, stems, the bines, grow rapidly from the branched rootstock to twine clockwise up and around anything that will support it. The greenish-yellow male and female flowers are small, in inflorescences on separate plants. The male flowers are on a loosely branched panicle; female flowers are short-stalked, without petals and brushlike. Cross-pollination is essential. To achieve it the male flowers issue a mass of pollen carried by the wind to be trapped on female flowers, which develop numerous overlapping scales or 'petals' that, as they mature, form the soft, near

Green hops ready to be picked.

oval ‘cones’. However, these are not the true ‘fruits’ of the Hop. Tiny achenes or ‘nuts’ within the cones are, one at the base of each scale or ‘petal’. They have no purpose other than to reproduce new plants; in fact, ‘seedless’ Hops were bred and have been grown for many years.

The ‘cones’ have resin glands between the ‘petals’ producing lupulin, a yellow, pollen-like secretion containing a substance, alpha acid. It is this that bitters the beer, acting also as a preservative so beer can be stored or transported without rapid deterioration. The flavour and aroma of beer derives from an essential oil in the ‘cones’. Brewers require hop varieties with a high alpha acid content, but the different hop varieties vary in this; some have a high alpha acid content, while others with less are grown instead for their pleasant aroma and distinctive flavour which they impart to certain beers.

Green hops, while being picked, due to the lupulin content, stain hands and clothes of pickers a dirty yellowish-green to near-black. This was removable, fortunately, with hot water, soap and vigorous scrubbing. Clothes worn, frequently the pickers’ oldest and tattiest were usually thrown away at the end of the season. The variety of clothing worn, especially the women’s hats, seemingly sometimes obtained from raiding grandma’s clothes cupboards, gave some of the pickers a picturesque appearance. But who cared? The reason for their apparel was ‘It’s good enough for hop picking.’

The Wild Hop was the original of two widely grown commercial varieties in Kent and

The three A's - the author between his mother, Annie (left) and a grandmother, Alice (right). Fred Scott's hop garden, Rainham, late 1930s.

Sussex, Fuggle and Goldings, although in curious circumstances. The first Fuggle hop bine is reputed to have been discovered at Horsmonden, then propagated about 1875 by a Richard Fuggle of Brenchley, Kent. Its flavour has been listed as 'earthy', 'grassy', 'sensuous' and 'moreish'. A Mr. Golding of 'Malling, Kent' is supposed to have discovered the first Golding hop bine on his farm in 1790. Realising its large 'cones' were superior to hops he was growing he propagated it, the variety eventually being commonly cultivated in the best hop soil areas. There were and are varieties bred for especial needs, this starting in the early 20th century when brewers were blending hop varieties together for a required type of brew. Some varieties produced a 'heavy' (abundant) early, main or late crop. Others suited different soils in the varied growing areas, or satisfied brewers' requirements for lupulin content, colour and flavouring characteristics. Even so, it was not until 1904 a breeding programme to find varieties disease and weather resistant was established. One example is the Whitbread Goldings Variety, in 1911, with a fragrant aroma and flavour for light beers. At Hoad's Farm, near Sandhurst, owned by the Nicholas family in the High Weald area of outstanding natural beauty, on the 76 acres of hop garden it is possible to see Whitbread Goldings Variety being grown with Goldings Early Choice, Bramling Cross, Progress, and Cobb's - all aroma varieties, also Pilgrim and Target, these being alpha hop varieties. The members of this family, however, are the last hop growers in Sandhurst, but have 12 acres of hops at Beckley, East Sussex. Encouragingly their hop gardens include one that was newly planted for 2005. The best time to see the hops is from June to September, but walkers MUST stay on the public footpaths. The farm has a five-square kilns Victorian

Measuring freshly picked hops from bins into pokes or greenbags. The men on the left and right are both holding up the open ends of a poke into which the measurers are about to tip their full bushel baskets of hops. Early 1900s. Photo: Author's collection.

brick and asbestos rectangular oasthouse in which they dry and bale their hops.

In addition to the two old varieties mentioned there were Apple Puddings, Pretty Wills, Golden Tips, Flemish Red Bine, Old Jones's Hop, Ruflers, Cobb's Hop, Amos' Early Bird, Grape Hop, to name a few. Some of the brewers also cultivated hop varieties especially required by them; others 'bought in' their hop needs; others did both.

And so the hops were cultivated in 'gardens', firstly trained up poles, later wires and coir string. Hops were picked from late August and through September into all sorts of containers, boxes, baths, upturned umbrellas, etc., eventually to be taken therein to a 'bin' or basket at the end of the row and tipped into it. From the 'bin' or basket the hops were 'measured' several times each day by the binman. Each bushel 'measured out' with the binman's bushel basket was counted as it was tipped into a poke held by an assistant. The final total of bushels 'measured', say 5 bushels, was noted in the binman's clerk's record book. The total was also noted on the card kept by each picker, as the payment received by the picker at the end of the season depended on the grand total stated on the card. When full, the poke, with others, was loaded on to a cart waiting nearby. In earlier times it was drawn by oxen, later by horses; later still the pokes were heaped on to a tractor-drawn trailer.

If the hop garden was near the oasthouse some of the supposed-to-be picking children standing at the picked ends of the hop rows after 'measuring' had finished, looking at the patient horses as the carts were loaded, sometimes could cadge a ride to the oasthouse

A cart load of pokes full of hops about to be transported to an oasthouse.
The photographer seems to have rounded up all the men in the area to be in the picture.
Card posted at Newington, a hop growing area near Sittingbourne, 1907. Photo: Author's collection.

lying among the filled cushiony pokes. A 'lucky' child would be sitting alongside the carter, looking at the rear ends of the horses and the hand-held reins being used by him to control, unless he had decided to walk beside the horses to the oasthouse. Arriving there the children jumped to the ground and ran back to their family, noisy with excited laughter about their "adventure". No worries then about protecting the children from falling off the cart or similar situations. If asked 'Want a ride?', we accepted - and told mum afterwards.

At the oasthouse the cartload of pokes was positioned under the open entrance doors of the first floor, where the assistant hands were waiting, the pokes being manhandled up and pulled into the entrance by them. 'Hands' was an old term for younger men who assisted the dryer so I use it herewith.

Many hop pickers saw the sun rise over the oasthouse and gardens and were glad it was probably going to be a dry day. Sign of the Sun Inn, Faversham.

Hoist Away

To manhandle the pokes of hops was possible in the smaller, only ground and first floor, oasthouses and not difficult. If the oasthouse had a second floor as a storage, or the roof space above the cooling floor was also a temporary storage for the pokes, before loading the hops on the kiln or kilns, then mechanical means, a hoist, was required to raise the pokes to the external door or doors at the second or third storey level.

The hoist comprised a projecting wood beam towards the end of which was fixed an iron pulley wheel on which ran the rope used to haul up the pokes. The hands attached the rope to the pokes then pulled on it to lift the pokes to the entrance. Alternatively, after one end was attached to some pokes the other end was tied to one of the horses taken out of the cart's shafts. The horse was then led far enough up the lane or track away from the oasthouse to lift the pokes to the entrance where the hands swung them inwards, then released the rope ready to be attached to the next pokes on the cart and so on.

The hoist was housed in a lucarne or bonnet gable over the eaves. Evidence where this survives is indicated now on oasthouses by there being a wooden structure extension, like a miniature shed, sometimes with small windows, but floorless and open at the bottom.

There are variations, basically a tiled or slated wooden extension to the roof with only brief, or no, sides, to house the hoist.

There were now-rarer versions in oasthouses with a hoist that supposedly made the latter more manoeuvrable. In the roof space a wooden frame was constructed in which was a large wooden wheel with an endless rope that turned the wheel and a smaller wooden drum, the rope carrying the load coiling around the drum and on to a roller above the entrance. This type was manually, not horse, operated. There still

The Marquess of Conyngham's rather eccentric oasthouse at Patrixbourne, Kent, in 1935, the pokes of hops being hoisted up by pulley in the lucarne. Photo: Author's collection.

survive many pulley wheels on oasthouse hoists that, alas, will never again haul up pokes of hops.

Unless being hauled up to the roof space for temporary storage receiving the pokes continued at the first floor until enough had been delivered to cover the drying floor or floors. On large acreage hop farms where a considerable quantity was regularly received the bigger oasthouses in use in this situation also had a covered wooden extension at one side, a raised platform with an open-slatted floor. Known as the greenstage on it the pokes of undried hops were stored until required for loading in the kiln or kilns. The open slats were important as they prevented the hops sweating or heating causing them to deteriorate.

Now was to take place the crucial task for which oasthouses waited almost a year - to dry the harvest of hops.

Now, the same view of the Patrixbourne oast in 2005.

Why Dry?

If they are not quickly and correctly dried hops soon decline in quality and decompose in storage. Green hops contain between 75% and 85% moisture by weight. When expertly dried this is reduced to about 6% to 10% as required. However, hops must not be allowed to become too dry and thus brittle because the pocketing would break them to flaky pieces. During cooling they are allowed to re-absorb some air moisture so are less brittle. If not used immediately following drying and pocketing but in storage until required hops' stored moisture content can also rise to 10% but is acceptable to brewers.

After drying hops are judged by colour and 'condition' - these eventually determining the hops' sale price. They should have a pleasant aroma, not too strong, with a high 'resin' content. Colour expected was and is either primrose-yellow or a straw-yellow, definitely never green indicating lack of ripeness and drying, nor too brown as this indicates over-ripeness and drying. The colour change of hop cones from green to a yellow was assisted by using sulphur (brimstone). On a long-handled, open tray, or small pan, rolled sticks of sulphur were placed and lit with some burning coal or coke, being put close to or on the kiln floor. Alternatively, sulphur sticks were put on top of the fire causing coal to have dancing blue flames. The sulphur dioxide gas rising from the sulphur passing through them affected the hops' colour causing the bleaching and helping preserve the hops for storage. Another method was a separate closed metal sulphur stove in which sulphur was burnt, the gas escaping upwards via a chimney. After 1980 sulphur was no longer used on the orders of the-then Hop Marketing Board and the brewers.

A drying term was 'full of condition', meaning on some hops being looked at closely, held to the nose and sniffed, then rubbed in the palm of the dryer's left hand with the thumb of the right hand, they were slightly clammy to the feel between fingers and thumb and emitted a bittersweet aroma, so were at the required quality. This test, known as 'rubbing down', indicated hops ready to be moved off the drying floor.

For centuries dryers had nothing more than their own judgement, what their fingers and thumbs, eyes and nose told them about colour, quality and aroma. Many of them, even after the introduction of a moisture-determining instrument to make the task 'easier', would not use 'that technical gadget', but still relied on their own test and experience. In addition, they claimed, with good reason, not all the hop varieties dried at the same speed, requiring a longer or shorter time, or to the same quality and colour. So it was necessary to know, again through experience, how the more frequently cultivated varieties differed in order to dry them successfully.

The Early Drying Story

The Flemish and Walloon weavers, dyers and other craft producers in the 16th century, having fled persecution in their own homeland, the Low Countries (Belgium and Netherlands), were allowed to settle in Canterbury and elsewhere in Kent and Sussex. They already had the practice of using hops in brewing a bitter beer for their own use. On emigrating to Kent they had to import hops required from where grown and dried in Flanders. The Flemish did not relish the ale created from malt liquor and drunk by the English. Instead of changing their taste to ale the reverse happened. The beer the Flemish drank began to find favour with the English, too. The Flemish also realised it would be more economical and easier if hops were grown in Kent rather than obtained by importing them. Encouraged by this demand from Flemish and English the first hop garden in Kent is thought to be one established at Westbere, near Canterbury, in 1520, where there is still a Hoplands Farm. By 1549 the 'new industrie of hop growing' was well established. Experts in hop cultivation had also arrived from the Low Countries to teach English would-be hop growers how to do so. But, of course, at this time oasthouses did not exist, although in 1585 a Rye brewery had a 'hoppehouse' but if a storage for imported hops only or county grown is unknown.

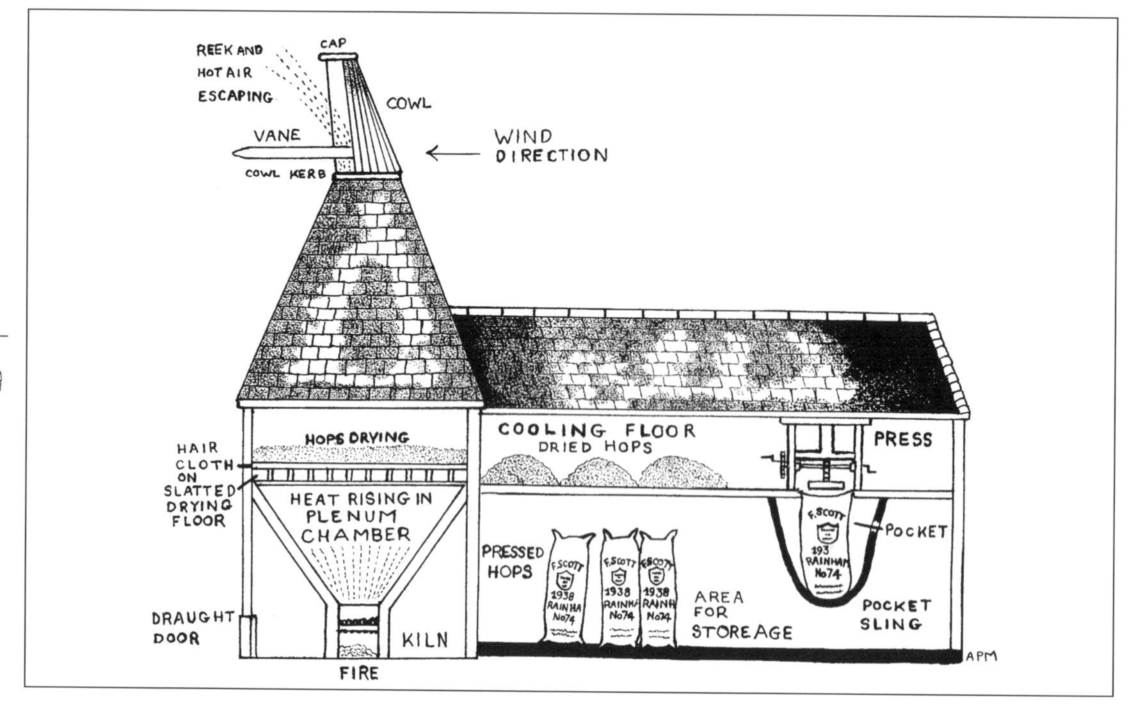

Section view of a basic single kiln 19th century oasthouse.

After being picked the green hops were laid out in the open air for the sun to dry them. This was not reliable or always successful because, as all pickers know, the sun does not regularly oblige in August and September, shining continuously for the weeks needed. Another method was to lay them in the roof space of buildings with chimneys and fireplaces so that the warmth from fires lit in the latter would encourage drying. A third method was to use malt drying kilns intended for that task. In fact none of these were sufficiently successful to deal with large quantities of hops coming from the increasing acreages of hop gardens. A method was required where the heat source was continual and it was controllable.

A watercolour 'Oasthouse interior, drying and pocketing hops' by C. Essenhigh Corke, 1906. It shows the oast's king post roof trusses above the side-winder press and man with a scuppet. The two men on the left appear to be taking pokes of hops to an upper floor for drying after which they were scuppeted down the chute to the cooling floor. Photo: Author's collection.

Reynolde Scot, the Hopping and Drying Pioneer

One of the first English writers on cultivating and drying hops was Reynolde Scot (1538-1599), interred in St. Mary's church, Smeeth, near Ashford, Kent. In 1574 he published his A Perfect Platform of a Hop Garden and Necessary Instructions for the Making and Maintenance Thereof, with Notes and Rules for Reformation of all Abuses commonly practised therein, very necessary and expedient for all men to have, which in any wise have to do with Hops. The title says it all. This was the first practical work published on hop cultivation in England and it was reputed to have done much to stimulate this in Kent and Sussex. It stayed the 'Bible' of hop growers for several centuries. By the time of its third reprint, in 1578, a flourishing hop growing industry was in production across southern England.

In Scot's lifetime the hop grower dried his own hops. Scot discussed the three methods. He was not happy with any of them. 'Some lay their hoppes in the sun to dry and this taketh away the state of the hoppes, contrary to the purpose of drying which is very prejudicial to the brewer.' His comment on drying in roof spaces was: 'Some used to dry their hops in a garret or upon the floor of a loft or chamber, in reproof thereof I must say that few men have room enough in their houses to contain a great quantity of multitude of hoppes so that the dust that will arise shall impair them, the chinks, crevices and open joints of your lofts, being not close byrthed (close boarded, boards flush against each other) will devour the seeds of them.' The result he says will be the hops 'be utterly spoiled in colour, in scent and verdure.' His advice is, when a necessity, 'If you have no oste dry them in a loft as open to the air as may be. Sweep, wash and rub the boards and let your broom reach to the walls and even to the roof of your loft. Stop the holes and chinks of your floor, lay the hoppes not half a foot thick and turn them once a day at least, by the space of two or three weeks. This done sweep them up into a corner of your loft and let them lye a day or more for yet there remaineth peril in packing (pocketing) them.' He didn't approve of the makeshift use of malt or corn-drying kilns either. The answer, Scot said, was artificial drying of hops in specially built buildings, 'an oste as they dry their hoppes upon at Poppering' that he had seen in use while travelling in Europe. Poperinghe, West Flanders, Belgium, is still situated in a hop cultivation area with a notable town Hop Museum.

Scot then describes how an oste should be built and he supplies woodcut illustrations explaining the various sections and their uses; 'The little timber-framed house would be 19 feet (about 5.79 m) in length and 8 feet (2.44 m) in width, with walls 9 feet (2.7 m) high, comprising three 'rooms' under a single roof. The dividing of the 'rooms' could be either brick, lowering the risk of fire, or timber covered with lath and plaster. In the ground floor middle room, the 'centrepart', a square room 64 square feet (5.9 sq.m), there was to be a 'furnace' or 'keele', 6 to 7 feet (1.8 to 2.1 m) in length, some 2 feet 6 inches (760 mm) in height and 13 inches (329 mm) internal width. The central 'furnace' was to have a pitched roof formed by two rows of bricks inclining against each other. So that the smoke, hot air and fumes could escape from the 'furnace' the latter's upper brick sides were built in the 'honeycomb' style of brickwork. The brickwork 'furnace' was 13 inches (325 mm) wide, 2 feet 6 inches (762 mm) long and 2 feet (609 mm) high. Approximately 5 feet (1.52 m) above the 'centrepart' ground floor 'furnace' was to be a drying floor. The latter comprising 1 inch (25 mm) square wood laths or 'slats' permanently positioned so there was a 1/4 inch (7 mm) space between them to allow the heat to rise in between the laths and through the hop layer and thus dry it. The laths were centrally supported by a strong wood beam under them and across the oste.

The green hops arrived at the 'forepart', the first room, the receiving room, 5 feet by 8 feet (1.52m by 2.44m). From the 'forepart' they were taken to the 'centrepart', the middle room, where they were spread upon the laths to a depth of about 18 inches (450mm). Apparently Scot did not use, or suggest, a haircloth between the laths and hops, but to lay hops directly on the bare laths. Perhaps he thought a haircloth would slow up drying. After being dried the hops were raked from the drying floor laths to the 'hynderpart', the third room, the cooling room. To allow the reek from the hops and 'furnace smoke' to escape there was probably an opening or several openings in the roof above these 'rooms'. The reek is humidity created by rapid water evaporation in the initial stages of drying.

As far as I know no hop oasthouse built to Scot's specifications now survives. An example with a likeness to his design - small, timber-framed, weather-boarded, with a single cowl built into the ridge of the roof - is at Little Golford Farm, Cranbrook, which may also be the smallest surviving oasthouse in Kent. It was rebuilt, about 1750, with twin brick 'furnaces' under the drying floor, using the timber and other materials from the earlier oasthouse. The cooling room was on the ground floor and boarded internally to about 4 feet high (1.2 m) in such a way as to form a container for the dry hops.

Oasthouse Developments

For about two hundred years Scot's design was used virtually unaltered. However, as growers had increased their hop garden acreages to meet rising demand this resulted in a larger quantity to be dried. The oasthouses' drying capacity at the time meant they were unable to cope with the situation. It was obvious drying capacity also had to be increased. Attempts were made to dry a greater depth of hops in one drying period, by an increase in the speed of the heated air flowing through the hops. But it was soon realised bigger, more efficient oasthouses, with more kilns, were the answer.

This increased demand for hops was surprising due to a law in the reign of James I (1603-1625), whereby using hops was banned, it being thought they had a harmful effect on the ..... beer! Prior to this, going back to Henry VI's reign (1422-1461) hop growing was forbidden, unhopped beer was known as ale and it was an offence to adulterate it. Someone uncharitably minded had even informed the authorities at Maidstone on a brewer there because, in 1426, he had used 'The abominable and unwholesome weed called a 'hoppe'. Physicians warned against using hops because any brew with them in could cause ailments from mental instability to limbs being deformed. Perhaps this was

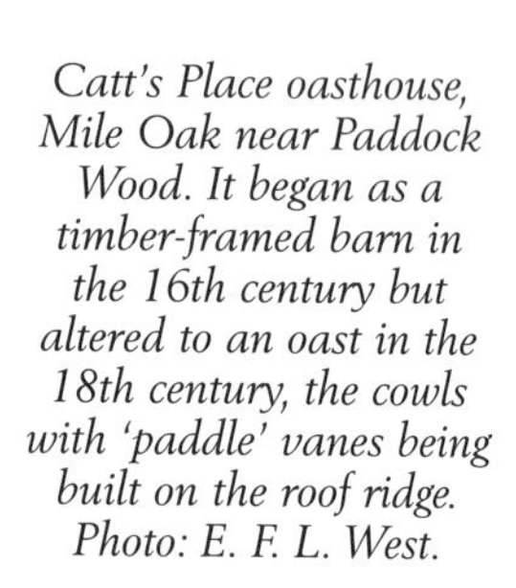

Catt's Place oasthouse, Mile Oak near Paddock Wood. It began as a timber-framed barn in the 16th century but altered to an oast in the 18th century, the cowls with 'paddle' vanes being built on the roof ridge. Photo: E. F. L. West.

meant to be protectionism for the ale trade. During Charles II's reign the campaign against the 'hoppe' continued. John Evelyn, eminent diarist-scientist who lived at Deptford supported it because he said valuable timber needed in Chatham to build navy ships was being used for hop poles. The snag to his complaint was that ships were mainly built of oak and elm; hop poles were almost always young sweet chestnut trees from Kent plantations. Nobody seems to have been bothered or hindered by these bans and laws. Bittering with hops continued. Incidentally, beer is made mainly from malted barley (barley that is wetted, allowed to sprout, then dried), hops, yeast, water and sometimes in certain beers sugar. Ale is malt liquor only.

The alteration of large barns, incorporating a fire with a drying floor above, to become an oasthouse, or the building of purpose-built oasthouses went ahead with speed in the later part of the 17th century. The former were usually owned by small hop growers with only one or two acres, the latter by wealthier, specialist hop growers. Those artisans with an acre of hops or less, among their various crops grown, or even a different craft or trade but grew some hops though without an oasthouse of their own, paid hop growers with an oasthouse to dry their hops for them.

In the 18th century it was also common to reposition the kilns when their numbers were to be increased. Some oasthouses continued to have a resemblance to a barn, with a single, or several, kilns at one end or centrally positioned. In other examples, during conversion, the internal square kiln was removed and placed on the exterior of the oasthouse allowing the entire interior to be for receiving green hops and cooling them. In some of the 18th century oasthouses, above the drying floor, in the roof space an inverted funnel was created by using a framing of lath and plaster walls, this funnel acting as a chimney at the summit of the roof ridge.

The larger, longer oasthouses that were built allowed several kilns to adjoin them along their length to deal with the greater quantity of hops, each kiln having its own roof, too. The roofs of these kilns were also of a pyramid shape that reduced upwards to their summit and an opening, the latter acting as a flue to encourage the needed draught from the kiln. The familiar white cowl (of which more later) was introduced to give, as one of its tasks, protection to this opening from the weather.

By the end of the 18th century oasthouses, had, through necessity, expanded from the single one kiln oasthouse with a small storage, to multiple oasthouses with several kilns and a corresponding single but much larger storage. Excellent examples are the range of oasthouses at the former Whitbread Hop Farm (now the Hop Country Park), Beltring, near Paddock Wood. Built 1894 the four large oasthouses with twenty cowls are reputed to be the largest oasthouse group in Britain.

In Kent by the 1900s new oasthouses were being constructed with a third storey, the latter used for receiving and the temporary storage of the green hops, while their second, middle floor, was used for cooling and pressing the dried hops, the ground floor being a storage for the pockets of dried hops. The first known example is believed to be the oasthouse, with high, brick-coned kilns, built on Down Farm, Lamberhurst, in 1876.

It will be noticed some oasthouses' walls have round iron straps and tie irons, or brick buttresses. These were incorporated or added to keep the wall structure supported and avoid its collapse. The cause may be the foundations of the oasthouse were not dug deep enough or sufficiently supportive and movement in the earth eventually caused the brickwork to crack or bulge.

Three-roundel brick kilns, 1910. Site unknown but size of the cowls, 'blinkers' style, indicates in Sussex.
Photo: Author's collection.

The Round Kilns

Until about the beginning of the 19th century the kilns had been built square in plan. Then the roundel kiln, round in plan, was introduced. An early example exists at Court Lodge Farm, Brook, near Wye, Kent, dated 1815. Involved in the change of shape was a John Read, (1760-1847) agent on the Smith-Marriott Estate, Horsmonden. In the south aisle of St. Margaret's church, Horsmonden, is a memorial bust to Read, placed there on his death by the Smith-Marriott family. He was also an 'inventor', in 1823 inventing a stomach pump, in 1840 a 'drowned man resuscitator', and, according to his memorial, 'many other implements for the benefit or relief of humanity'. While also a gardener on the Estate from about 1796 he had experimented with stoves for heating greenhouses. This led him to the task of drying hops and to introduce the round kiln, claimed to 'achieve extra space, strength and economical expenditure.'

Read's design was published in 1833, the publisher, J.C. Loudon, stating: 'The circular form for the kiln has been adopted by Mr. Read because it contains a greater area than any other with the same quality of exterior walling and because both the walls and roof can be made stronger than they can in any rectangular form, with fewer materials. Hence

The three-roundel kilns Church Oast among the orchards at Newington-by-Sittingbourne in the early 1960s, a scene much changed. Taken from the tower of St. Mary's church.

while the circular kilns possess more strength and durability than the rectangular ones the expense of construction is less.'

The main advantage of the round kiln, known also as roundel kiln, over the square kiln was also surmised to be that in square kilns the hops accrued in the kiln's drying floor corners did not receive enough heat to dry them sufficiently. Whereas in round kilns, not having any corners and with assumed better draught, all the hops supposedly received the same heat.

A hopper principle for drying was adopted from the square kilns to fit in the roundel kilns. The open fires were situated in the centre of the roundel circle and were stoked and fuelled from the circular passage inside the kiln's wall formed by arched brickwork as a sort of inverted cone-shaped plenum chamber under the drying floor. At the Wye College Agricultural Museum the oasthouse there has one preserved in section.

It is surprising round kilns were accepted to be cheaper to build because the tiles used to cover the roof had to be specially made or, alternatively, slates adjusted to fit. Even so, when a new kiln was required it was built round. The change back came about 1875 when the construction of new, round kilns was abandoned in a return to favour of the square kiln design when Mr Read was proved wrong and it became obvious from studying comparative costs there was little difference in cost of construction of round and square kilns. In some examples it had even been cheaper to build a square kiln instead of a round kiln. It was also noted there was no advantage in the air flow and drying heat distribution in the round kiln over the square kiln. So, from about this date new oasthouses were square.

Hall and Russell writing in 1911 commented: 'The kilns or oasts used for drying hops form the most characteristic feature in the landscape in Kent and East Sussex. The older kilns were round, nowadays they are usually built with square floors.'

A Mix of Oasthouses

It will be noted when looking at oasthouses in Kent and Sussex no two are exactly the same, due, in the main, to changes made in their structural existence to meet needs at the time. I think this individualistic character of them adds to their charm. There are examples where several round kilns stand close to or among several square kilns, indicating perhaps the round kilns were added later. A possibility is the round kilns are early examples and the square kilns were built later. There survive oasthouses that are entirely separate from the owner's farm or they are now part of a complex of vari-aged buildings. In some examples the storage for the pockets of hops may be an add-on, or separate, small rectangular building. There may also be a small single-storey building nearby added on to the oasthouse exterior wherein was stored fuel for the fires.

There are kilns whose roofs are noticeably taller than those of neighbouring kilns and the reason for this was to gain as much benefit as possible from the wind. Some oasthouse designs are obviously the whim of the owner-farmer who had them built. One at Patrixbourne in Victorian orné style, constructed in bricks for the Marquess of Conyngham in 1869 is magnificently eccentric in appearance. It has three 18 feet

Thruxted Oast. The two chestnut trees on the right survive, too. (Kent County Journal, Summer, 1934). The prize winning drawing by Nicoleta Pomfret (see page 45).

diameter (5.5m) brick roundel kilns along its rear wall, purlins (longitudinal beams in the roof resting on the principal rafters and carrying the common rafters), also having wall brackets at the gable ends of the storage supporting the curious barge boards that support spike finials. Built into the roof at the front are four gable and dormer windows and a lucarne, with a pulley, these dormers having upswept roofs. In the brickwork is the date-stone with the crest of the Marquess. When not used for its original purpose or storage the vast cooling floor and storage, 75 feet long (22.9m) by 23 feet wide (7.0m), could soon be, and was, cleared to hold dances and other functions. Since 1988 it has been two dwellings.

Thruxted Oast, Thruxted Lane, Mystole, Chartham, is unusual in plan, with five two-storey, parallel, rectangular oasthouses, each having a tiled roof used as extra storage and a cowl astride one end of the roof ridge. Standing also parallel to the Lane they form one large building, a hoist being on the east side. The Oast was originally part of the nearby Mystole estate (Queen Anne period house with Victorian additions), owned by the Pomfret family when members of my family were footmen and the head gardener there late 19th century, early 20th century. Thruxted Farm, also part of the Mystole estate with a tenant, was sold to a farmer, Tom Scutt, in 1942, his family planting hops through the adjoining valley. The Oast remained in use until 1967, then sold in 1972 for conversion to dwellings. In 1934 Kent County Journal held a competition for children to draw an oasthouse. The late Nicoleta Pomfret, known personally to the author, 14-year-old

The large weatherboarded oasthouse at Elbridge Farm, Littlebourne, with brick-and-tiled roundel kilns.

daughter of Virgil Pomfret, then owner of Mystole, drew Thruxted Oast and was highly delighted to win second prize, five shillings (25p). Thruxted Oast is believed to have been one of the first to install power driven fans, perhaps the reason for there only being two cowls, but three louvres in Nicoleta's drawing, later the cowls being all returned for appearance reasons when the Oast was converted.

In Bekesbourne Lane, Littlebourne, it is daunting to realise a large, partly weatherboarded, brick oasthouse, comprising several dwellings, is teetering on the bank edge of the Nailbourne, a shallow river flowing through the village. Consisting of two square kilns and one rare octagonal kiln the water literally laps their foundations in the picturesque scene.

The appearance of oasthouses is also enhanced by the materials from which they were built. As stated, the early oasthouses, in the 16th and 17th centuries, were timber-framed with ragstone foundations and clad on the exterior with horizontal boards that were usually black tarred to waterproof them. The interior was covered with wattle and daub - wattle being a rough, interwoven wickerwork made of ash and hazel rods, fitted to the oasthouse's framework, plastered on its surface with daub, a glutinous mixture of clay, animal hair, chopped straw and cow dung, so, when spread over the wattle a flat, wall-like surface was created.

A change came in the mid-to-late 18th century into the mid-19th century, with oasthouses being built of brick and wood, the ground floor of bricks, the upper storey timber-framed. On the exterior the upper storey was weatherboarded with horizontal flat boards either painted white or tarred black, an alternative cladding being horizontal battens on which were hung or nailed clay tiles. The interior of the upper storey was covered with flat, horizontal boards, too.

Another change was caused in 1784 when a tax was placed on bricks by the government. To avoid it, not surprisingly, various other materials were introduced to build oasthouses. One was flints. When quarries were dug in chalk areas to obtain chalk to make lime for liming farmland and other purposes flints were found in it. What was versatile to build numerous castles and churches in Southern England, or part of the structure, was thought versatile to build oasthouses. Or was it? Not entirely. A problem might have been that flints, although they could be knapped, i.e., have one side cut flat, the shiny outward side seen, they were in natural variable shapes and sizes. Even when bedded in mortar the wall would not have been as strong as needed. This was overcome by having full width brickwork rows, comprising several bricks per layer at periodic intervals in the walls made otherwise of flints. To give more strength chips of flint were pushed into the mortar joints between the flints in flint walls. This can often also be seen done in flint walls of churches.

The corners or quoins of the square kilns were also in some cases bricks, but more often large blocks of Kentish ragstone, a greenish or greyish-brown rock found in the county. When quarried ragstone rocks were used bedded in mortar for entire walls of oasthouses the walls had to be built thicker to obtain the required strength, too, the corners or quoins of the walls being of bricks. A roundel kiln with ragstone walls is at Mote Farm, Ightham.

Where it was available in Kent and Sussex dark yellow sandstone was used, again with brick quoins. An oasthouse, now a dwelling, The Old Oast in Stream Lane, Hawkhurst, has two unusual octagonal kilns built with sandstone ashlar (hewn blocks). A few early oasthouses in the area were also built with ironstone, a dark brown rock occurring in the Weald of Kent. Very unusual, perhaps unique, is the two-roundel kilns, now a dwelling, Tilden Oast, near Headcorn, one of its roundels being built with brownish-grey Bethersden marble quarried in Kent. It is perhaps surprising that as part of the county sits on considerable depths of chalk, even though it can be an unstable material, more oasthouses were not built with it. One that partially was is the 19th century Street Farm Oast, Boxley, now a dwelling, that has chalk blocks, as well as flint, ragstone and red brick walls. The chalk and flints most likely came from chalkpits cut into the North Downs nearby.

In 1850 the bricks tax was scrapped and oasthouse builders from then on used red, yellow or vari-coloured handmade clay bricks laid in lime mortar, later machine-made sand and lime bricks in cement mortar were used. A student of different types of brickwork - English bond, Flemish bond, English garden wall bond, Flemish garden wall bond, with different stretchers and headers - will find them all in oasthouse walls in Kent and Sussex. Similarly, with roof interiors of the storage. The early examples of Scot's lifetime and for

A side view of the oasthouse cowls and vanes, at Elbridge Farm, Littlebourne.

a period after him had a single roof with a tie beam and rafters. When oasthouses increased in size the double-roof style was brought in, this also having extra horizontal beams supported by the main rafters increasing the roof strength. In the 19th century the triple or framed roof style was introduced with frames or trusses and king posts to support the weight of the large roofs.

There were also variations of all these styles for local requirements, such as when altering the roof area for extra storage.

Until the early 19th century roof beams were obtained from hewn and seasoned oak, perhaps from woodland not far from where the oasthouse was being constructed. Oak, because it is heavy, was eventually replaced during the 19th century by Scots pine or other softwoods available that were lighter but also cheaper. Fortunately today in many examples where oasthouses have been sensitively converted, especially to dwellings, these beams and other timberwork have been retained, suitably restored where necessary, preserved to enhance the property.

Following the first oasthouses the roofs of later storages were and still are covered by Kent Peg tiles, these being handmade of clay. At first they were kept in position with wood pegs upon laths, later by galvanised nails. Alternatively, the roofs were and are covered with slates, each kept in position with two galvanised nails on battens.

When looking up into the roof of a square or round kiln it is realised what a work of art it is. I am not qualified to state how they were actually constructed, from the wall plate, rafters, hips, purlins and jacks of a pyramid-shaped roof of the square kiln, or from the wall plate, rafters and ring of the cone roof of the roundel/round kiln, but certainly skilled were the craftsmen who created them. The square kiln roofs were covered with slates or tiles. Internally the roofs were then lathed and plastered.

From around the mid-19th century the cone-shaped kiln roofs were instead built of bricks, a half-brick thick. Sometimes the bricks were additionally covered with cement rendering externally to make them extra watertight, but then were not plastered internally. The cement rendering might also be coated with a mixture of tar and pitch applied hot to seal it and increase watertightness.

It is also noteworthy when looking at oasthouses there is a multiplicity of styles through the centuries in the creating of the arches and lintels over their doors and windows, also the other openings in their walls, such as air vents. Sometimes they are curved, sometimes horizontal, of brick, ragstone or wood. The doors and windows themselves have also undergone changes. Some doors are basically simple, of several wide vertical boards held by three horizontal boards, other doors having a substantial frame, several vertical boards, held by horizontal boards between the latter being angled boards.

There were and still remain in use a variety of hinges on which the doors were hung, the heavier the door the more substantial and stronger the iron hinges used. To secure them several types of wood or metal lock were used on internal and external doors.

Windows range from wooden uprights in the otherwise open windows of early oasthouses, to horizontal wood louvres, cast iron window frames with small panes of glass, wood casement windows with panes of glass to recent steel casement windows and pivoted large glass plane windows. To close the open, no glass windows in wet or windy weather they were fitted with hinged wood shutters. These also closed the oasthouse windows for protection in winter. The windows in the storage were small because too much sunlight was harmful to the dried hops, thus the interior of some of the oasthouses' cooling floors were made gloomy. The metal examples used on oasthouse conversions today are there for security reasons.

When artificial light was needed the first method used candles housed in lanterns for some sort of safety in the dryness of an oasthouse. These were sometimes supplemented or replaced by oil lamps. The introduction of paraffin meant the development of the safer 'hurricane' lamp, widely used in oasthouses in the late 19th century and early 20th century. When electricity became practical for illumination farmers installed their own generators driven by Lister oil engines to supply to their farm buildings including the oasthouse. However, it was not until the mid-20th century that isolated rural farms were eventually linked to the national electricity supply.

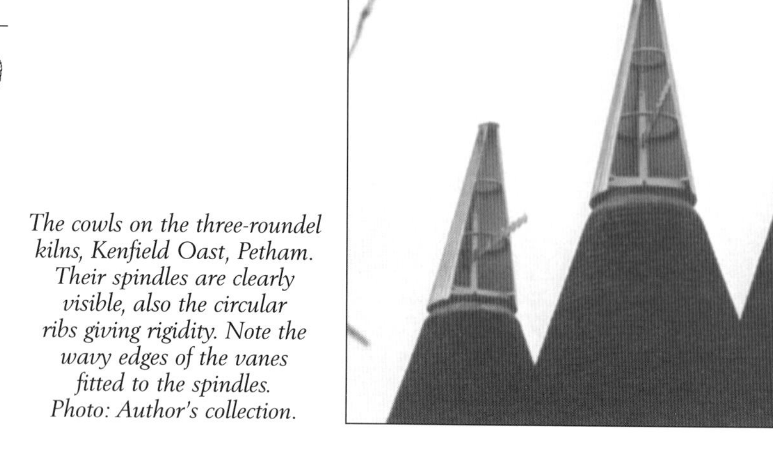

The cowls on the three-roundel kilns, Kenfield Oast, Petham. Their spindles are clearly visible, also the circular ribs giving rigidity. Note the wavy edges of the vanes fitted to the spindles. Photo: Author's collection.

The Cowls, the Cowls...

The square and round kilns, with a pyramidal or cone-shaped roof, formerly only had an opening at the latter's summit to emit the air and its reek. Then at the end of the 18th century the cowl, sometimes known as the hood, was developed to protect this opening as one of its purposes. These familiar cowls, with their pointing vanes when seen in the landscape are instantly recognised by county-born Kent and Sussex people. Perhaps more than anything else they indicate to the viewer they are in a hop-growing area or it formerly was so.

One purpose of the cowls was and is to prevent the entry of rain into the kiln. Another purpose was to ventilate the kiln, being thus shaped so the cowl by means of its vane turned away from it and had its boarded 'back' or 'spine' to the wind, preventing downdraughts into the kiln, so the moisture-heavy air was extracted from within the kiln, this air being drawn up from the hops layer on the drying floor. In other words, the kiln roof and cowl created a vacuum so a constant draught of warm air passed through the drying hops. However, a problem could be that the sucking up of the air by the cowl meant the stability of the required draught depended on the weather conditions, not always favourable and thus the hop dryers were then not in overall control of the drying.

As with many other useful developments who the local craftsman or men were who 'invented' and made the first cowl and installed it is now unknown. More likely it is one of those objects that evolved according to the use of the kiln, whether for malt, hops or corn. In John Thorpe's Custumale Roffeuse published 1782 he used an illustration of a cowl on the ridge of the former Chapel of St. Katharine, at Shorne, Kent, this Chapel being one of several religious purpose buildings that had been converted to other uses, St. Katharine's being to hop drying.

A kiln's cowl is an inclined cone with, usually, one side open for less than half its circumference. From close to its base, or a near-central position, it has the projecting horizontal vane, known also as the pointer, finger or flyboard, serving as a 'rudder' in positioning the cowl. They vary in height and from the ground may appear small. Early examples were smaller than those in use today, but now range from 5 feet high (1.52m) to a surprising 14 feet high (4.3m), but the average is from about 9 feet high (2.7m) to 10 feet high (3.05m).

The cowl is not as simple an object as it looks. It comprises in its parts, a spine, some ribs, a collar, spindle, wedge, tie bar, a spigot, iron sleeve, metal stays, boards and support beams.

Basically, the two support beams are fixed into the main rafters of the kiln roof at a position several feet from the kiln's summit. On the top edge of the upper of the two support beams is a fixed metal plate into which fits a metal spigot, the other end of the spigot being forced into the lower end of a central, vertical beam, the spindle. On the upper part of this vertical beam, the spindle, the cowl is mounted. The spigot is what allows the cowl to rotate. At the very summit of the kiln roof is a ring or curb and to the latter is fixed several metal stays that are part of a metal collar that keeps the spindle vertical. The vane itself is passed through a mortice in the spindle and fixed to the spine of the cowl. If the vane is at a near-central position in the cowl two metal rods fitted to it at about a halfway point along the vane and extending back to where fitted on the cowl, are intended to support the vane. The cowl is made of boards that overlap each other from the spine to the cowl's open side. The cowl's upper and lower wood ribs are semi-circular and give it rigidity. Occasionally, however, some cowls have completely circular ribs and the vane is attached to the lower rib. The cowl boards' narrow top ends are nailed to a block and upon this is the flat wood cap giving some protection to the block from the weather.

Cowls in the past were made by the village wheelwright; today it is a specialist craft task. They are the same in design in Kent and Sussex, having the characteristic flat top cap. In the Midlands and other hop growing areas the cowls are pointed and nicknamed 'witches' hats.' A regional variation in Sussex is the outside edge of the cowls on each side of the opening sometimes have parallel boards. Similar examples were occasionally

The regional variation of Sussex cowls where the opening has parallel boards, which some wag once said made it look as if the cowls had blinkers. Leafwood Oast, Bells Yew Green Road on a route to Frant. Photo: Norman Elms.

also used on Weald of Kent oasthouses.

The last oasthouse to be built in Kent with a revolving cowl on the kiln, not louvred ventilators, is believed to be the Clockhouse Farm Oast, Hunton, of 1928.

Should the cowl become fixed in one direction, perhaps because the spindle is stuck and unable to rotate and move the cowl, the strength of the wind coming from a different direction, especially gale strength could damage, even destroy the cowl. The usual consequence is the cowl's boards and spine break away from the spindle, to lean at an alarming, unnatural angle. Or the cowl's boards may 'spring' apart. To avoid this mishap owners who maintain their example themselves ensure the spigot and associated parts are regularly greased and oiled.

If a cowl is damaged because of its high position it usually cannot be repaired in situ, but it has to be taken down. The cowl's boards and vane are dismantled from the spindle and lowered to the ground manually or by crane. Repairs done the cowl is hauled up the side of the kiln roof again manually or by crane, then fitted on to the spindle. Should the spindle, spigot and its metal plate be damaged, maybe so the spindle is no longer true vertically, then the whole structure has to be dismantled and rebuilt.

It is the vanes that allow the oasthouse's owner some scope for artistic licence. Familiar on Kent cowl vanes is the county badge of Kent, a rampant horse. At Sheerland Farm, Pluckley, a ragstone oasthouse, built 1838, has its vanes bearing the horse passant sable,

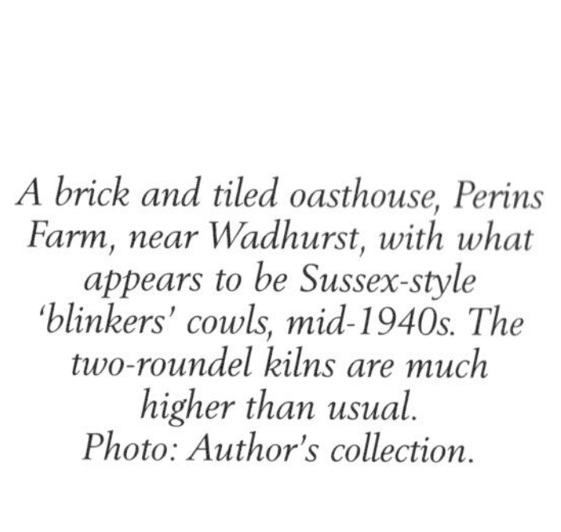

A brick and tiled oasthouse, Perins Farm, near Wadhurst, with what appears to be Sussex-style 'blinkers' cowls, mid-1940s. The two-roundel kilns are much higher than usual. Photo: Author's collection.

the Dering family crest, as the farm was part of their estate. The six vanes each have a conspicuously large black Shire horse made of iron fitted to them. At Little Scotney Farm near Lamberhurst the four-roundel kilns oasthouse, built 1871, still in use for its original purpose, has cowls that individually bear the letters A, H, W and E, believed to represent the names Arthur, Henry, William, Edward, the four sons of Edward Hussey who lived at Scotney Castle from 1831 to 1894.

Sometimes the owner had and has on the vane a symbol of his rural or sporting interest, a racehorse, a trotting horse, a huntsman on horseback with hounds and the fox, too, but on a vane of its own on another cowl. The oasthouse's new use may also be similarly symbolised, a blacksmith's anvil, a pottery jug or pot, etc. The former Wakeley's oasthouse alongside Rainham's railway station has steam engines, one per vane, dating from the time when converted from an oasthouse to a community centre. Upon the single roundel cowl vane on the Kent Wildlife Trust's Bough Beech oasthouse centre is depicted a hop bin and two people involved in hop measuring from it.

The vane may have a pointed or spike end, but some are carved as a pointing finger, arrowhead or a spade. The top and underside edges of the vane are usually straight. Exceptions are wavy on these edges. An example of the latter is the three roundel kilns oasthouse, Kenfield Oast, Petham, Kent, now a dwelling.

For some unknown reason, perhaps to make the cowls conspicuous so wind direction can

An aerial view, from a hot-air balloon, of the former Whitbread hop farm, Beltring, near Paddock Wood, now the Hop Farm Country Park. Photo: Hop Farm Country Park, Paddock Wood.

be determined from afar, they were traditionally painted white. That rule still continues today among owners.

One exception is at Chart Court Oast, Little Chart, Kent, where the four-roundel kilns oasthouse has red and green cowls. Two are painted vertically red-green-red, each section being a third of the cowl, and two are painted vertically green-red-green, also each section being a third of the cowl. The vanes are the same colour as the outer thirds of the cowls, the cowl interiors being white. As the oasthouse is walked around the cowls alternate in colour scheme, i.e., red-green-red, green-red-green, etc. A reputed reason for being thus painted is emerald and flame were the racing colours of Mrs. Edith Chester Beatty, wife of a Chester Beatty, (1875-1968), wealthy American businessman who took British nationality in the 1930s both living at nearby Calehill Park, Little Chart and who, as part of their estate, possibly owned Chart Court Farm and Oast, too. The oasthouse was probably built in 1858 as datestones on two kiln walls state 'R.C. 1858' and 'F.C. 1858'. In August, 1944, nearby St. Mary's church was destroyed by a doodlebug that damaged the oasthouse and farmhouse. In 2000 the oasthouse was purchased and restored but as a private dwelling as it still is. As the oasthouse is listed the cowls must stay red and green.

Poets have gone into raptures about the white cowls when several were to be seen, likening them to a fleet of white-sailed yachts at sea, or the outstretched necks and bodies of large white birds. When the array of cowls on the Hop Farm oasthouses at Beltring are seen gleaming white in sunshine it has to be admitted the poets have a relevant point.

Then... beyond the ruins of St. Mary's Church, Little Chart, destroyed by a flying bomb on 16th August 1944, is framed the three cowls of Chart Court Oast, war damaged but restored shortly afterwards.
Photo: Author's collection.

Beech Court Gardens, former 19th century brick and weatherboarded oasthouse. The cone roof of the roundel kiln has been removed and the original cooling floor roof extended.

Chart Court Oast, Little Chart, with its unique painted cowls, near to St. Mary's Church bombed during the war. Photo: Paul Gardiner, Chart Court Oast.

An end view of the Patrixbourne oasthouse.

Thruxted Oast today, east side, showing the lucarne and hoist pulley wheel.

Oasthouses in Wartime

An exception to cowls being always white was in the 1939-45 war when some of the large oasthouses in areas near to aerodromes, gunsites and other wartime installations were not only painted brown and green to help camouflage them, but the cowls were painted black to make them less conspicuous and difficult to recognise as navigation points by enemy aircrews. Several were damaged by bombs dropped nearby. A row of huts and other buildings could from the air appear to have a military use to be bombed. Even though in some areas the huts were also painted black, or brown and green, to try to camouflage them into their surroundings there were several instances of German fighters machine-gunning hop gardens, oasthouses, huts and other buildings, the pickers in the hop gardens, too. This assumption of military use would have been correct with Whitbreads Hop Farm, as it then was, Paddock Wood, in 1944, when troops and heavy vehicles were stationed there for the D-Day invasion of France. Prior to this the War Office had requisitioned some of the oasthouses there to house the 1st Battalion, the Queen Victoria Rifles, from 1st November, 1939, until 10th May, 1940. There is a memorial at the Hop Farm to the men of the Rifles who later lost their lives in France or were captured.

Now... the same scene today in 2005. Photo: Paul Gardiner, Chart Court Oast, Little Chart.

In oasthouses at Chestfield, near Herne Bay, known as North Oast and South Oast, when they were converted into dwellings postwar on the beams of the upper floor were discovered names of Home Guard men who had spent time there inscribed on the beams.

A wooden lucarne off the former oasthouse off Roper Road, Canterbury, that has its bottom edges in the style of a valance (pelmet), common on railway station buildings. Its use here is not surprising as it is close to Canterbury West station.

A large brick and slated former two-square kilns oasthouse, now business and dwellings use, off Roper Road, Canterbury.

The Drying Floor

Having previously mainly discussed the structure of the oasthouses and various developments through the centuries we arrive at the internal parts they all have or had.

In Reynolde Scot's day the drying floor comprised an area of laths nailed on to the floor's timber joists, with a quarter of an inch space between each lath, to allow air through them. On the lath area the green hops were spread. The undried hops being natural size could not fall through the spaces in between the laths before and while drying. As they did so, however, they shrank so the brittle hops could disintegrate and the 'petals' drop between the laths to the kiln below. This situation was soon changed from Scot's method by the introduction of the 'hair cloth', laid like a carpet covering over the laths, but it was of a loosely interwoven material so the heated air from below was not restricted.

In 1681, in his Systems Agriculture, an author named Worlidge advised oasthouse owners 'To contain the hair of your oost tack round the same about the edges.'

By the late 18th century using a 'haircloth', an open weave mat of horsehair, was common. The horsehair cloth would have been supplied by a tradesman in the local village or nearest market town. In 1748 the tenant hop grower of Tatlingbury Farm, Capel, near Tonbridge, paid £2.11 shillings to a Stephen Potter who supplied him with '34 yards of oast hair at 1 shilling and 6 pence a yard.'

Horsehair was used because it was not affected or damaged by fumes from the sulphur or heat from the fire. It was strong enough to support the weight of the hops but allowed air through it. This horsehair mat was used into recent times because modern fabric materials soon deteriorated in these conditions. In some of the oasthouses a 'lifter cloth', also made of loosely woven material, and suspended from hooks on the drying floor wall, was situated to cover sections of the horsehair mat. After they were dry the lifter cloth with the hops on it was picked up section by section to convey the hops more easily to the cooling floor. In the 19th century the quarter-inch gap between the laths of Scot's time was widened to one inch to increase heated air flow to the hops on the horsehair mat or lifter cloth.

To ensure they were equally drying over the area of the drying floor the dryer and his hands turned the hops regularly with long-handled, wide-headed, wooden, blunt-tined rakes. Alternatively a blunt-tined wooden hop fork, like a digging fork, was also used to turn over the hops and ensure they were spread evenly. The hop fork was also used to raise up the hops so they stayed loose, did not bear down and become compacted together, this task being known as 'hovering up'.

A few of the square kilns had a means of enabling the dryer to move over the drying hops to check them which avoided having to step among and possibly damage hops. This comprised several wood planks the width of the kiln as a platform, there being wheels at each end of the planks. The wheels moved along rails on the side walls. By pulling on a rope secured to each end wall the dryer hauled himself and the platform on which he stood across the hops, to bend or kneel down and check the hops underneath the platform, then to stand up and haul himself further over the hops until all were checked, upon which he pulled himself back to the kiln end wall from where he started.

The late 19th and early 20th century, with the re-introduction of square kilns, allowed the introduction of a different method, the roller haircloth. The green hops were first spread on the haircloth and dried. On drying a wooden roller as wide as the kiln was turned by hand-cranked handles and as it was so the dried hops on the cloth passed over the roller and automatically fell onto a lifter cloth on which the hops were carried to the cooling room. It was claimed the use of a roller horsehair mat meant it reduced the breaking of the dry hops when at their most brittle stage after drying and the hops could be unloaded quicker from the drying floor to the cooling room floor.

Later, in some oasthouses, the horsehair mat on the drying floor was replaced with narrow-mesh wire fixed to the laths. An example was Crawford's oasthouse near Upchurch on which the author walked as a youth. An alternative to mat and wire in a few oasthouses was the drying floor being tiled, the glazed tiles being perforated.

Dried and cooled hops waiting to be pressed in pockets - side-winder press on left, by birch broom, above which is a hurricane lamp. In the centre the man is holding a scuppet, next to him the man has a hop rake. 1905. Photo: Author's collection.

Time Involved

Where an oasthouse had several kilns hop drying was a continuous process. The pickers would have been in the gardens from sunrise and as a result of their labours the hops that had been picked would have been 'measured', transported and delivered to the oasthouse early to mid-morning, quantity depending on how large the garden and number of pickers working in it.

Each drying floor would be immediately loaded with their layer of hops. The hands sometimes did this shirtless and vestless due to the heat already rising, similarly 'dressed' being the men who stoked the fires in the kilns.

How long the hops stayed on the drying floor could be as short as six hours to as long as twenty hours, but between nine to eleven hours was more normal. If the average time was the latter to dry the hops the drying floors would be unloaded about mid-evening, the hops being moved on to the close-boarded cooling floor. The drying floors would again be loaded simultaneously with green hops that had been picked from mid-morning to mid-afternoon, 'measured' and transported to the oasthouse in the afternoon. Unloading the drying floors, moving the hops to the cooling floor and re-loading the drying floors with the second picking took between two to three hours, again depending on the quantity of hops, number of kilns with fires ready, also sometimes the amount of labour of hands available.

The first dried hops moved onto the cooling floor stayed thereon for an average of seven to eight hours, which meant it was in the early hours of the following morning when the hops were ready to be moved into the pockets. This latter task could also take two to three hours and when finished the cooling room floor was bare, but by this time the second picking of hops was dried and ready to be moved onto the cooling floor. So this routine went on day by day, night by night, during the hop-picking season.

The Dryers

In total control of all this drying procedure was the head dryer. He had to ensure the fires in the kilns were at the correct temperatures for drying. He had to know when to increase or reduce the temperature according to the condition of the hops and other circumstances such as changes in the weather. He decided when the hops were sufficiently dried to unload the drying floor or floors and move the hops to the cooling floor, then, when cool enough, to pack in the pockets. The head dryer would move about among each layer of drying hops by day and night, poking with his hands and fingers, having the hops turned here, turned there, to obtain an even drying over each entire layer.

It was the head dryer, when an oasthouse's drying floor and cooling floor were full for the day with drying and cooling hops, who made the decision, sent via a message to the 'measurer' and binmen in the hop gardens 'Pull no more bines'. Some pickers were not usually sorry and all children certainly wanted to hear it. This meant, after the hop bines already pulled down had been picked of their hops and then put in the bins, the weary pickers and their wearier children could go home.

Richard Church describes the scene in the oasthouse vividly in his Kent : 'The dryer, his

The head dryer, second left, holds a scuppet to move the cooled hops in rows to the side-winder press, where a hand waits to operate it. The man extreme left is standing on the short ladder formerly used in 'treading' hops. 1906. Photo: Author's collection.

eyes bloodshot with heat and fumes, his skin smeared with the bine stain, moves about half drugged by the perfume of the shrinking pods. The light from the fire throws grotesque shadows up the circular walls, menacing shapes that leap and bow and mow like gigantic bats flickering around the more substantial objects. The scent of the drying hops is unforgettable but it cannot be described. It floats out over the countryside from the open hoods at the top of the kilns; a keen, half-medicinal tang, with something bracing about it, yet old-fashioned and reminiscent of moods, moments and far-off things that we strive vainly and intensely to remember as we stand at some lane end or under the shelter of a wood where the scent lingers...'

As far back as 1798 William Marshall referred to this and the 'kilnman', a farm worker of much experience enduring scorching heat, dusty sweating in the heavy stoking of the fires, draughts of chilly night air, the acrid fumes from the sulphur, the sticky blackness of the hop resin and the fight to resist sleep, plus bloodshot eyes rimmed with tiredness, face as black as a chimney sweep.

Most old dryers had had experience of the task since they were young men and drying hands themselves. The farmers trusted them. On a head dryer's judgement depended a good or poor price for the hops. When a dryer retired he, even in old age, often came out of retirement to dry his former employer's hops in the oasthouse he knew so well. He also knew the importance of the task and knowing, too, he was mortal, he passed on his skill to his hands; a dryer's assistant being known as an oast hand.

Richard Hayes refers to this: '29 August, 1765. Began hopping this day at noon..... My dryer is Old Styles. T. Higgins sits up with him to learn.... The old man is almost worn out.' It is easy to imagine the number of 'hopping' seasons 'Old Styles' had worked in.

The head dryer could sometimes be recognised by being the oldest man in the oasthouse. Frequently, too, he wore some sort of hat or other headgear different to those worn by his younger hands, the latter often sporting flat caps.

The head dryer and his hands 'slept' with the hops, snatching short naps rather than longer periods asleep. They made up a pile of empty hop pokes, or whatever was reasonably comfortable and available, as a bed. Sometimes they had the luxury of old mattresses on an available space or sacks stuffed with fresh straw probably available from the earlier cutting of the corn harvest. Old armchairs and similar furniture were also lugged inside in lieu of 'beds'. No blankets were required. They catnapped in their clothes, the kiln's heat sufficing to keep them warm. This routine of course meant the dryer and his hands could not go home and come back again as a regular hours' job. It was a twenty-four hour task, tending the fires and draught doors, regulating the temperature, overseeing the hops.

The dryer and his hands also ate with the hops. Some dryers who were especially particular about their job, did not even cook their meals on the kiln fire. They and their hands did this outside in the open so any smoke from their cooking fire did not affect drying hops. Fortunate were the dryers and hands where the oasthouse was near their homes, or at least not too far away, so the dryer's and hands' families could bring them food and refreshment at relevant times.

Dryers and hands aptly and wisely drank large quantities of beer or other liquid refreshment by day and night; very necessary in the conditions under which they worked. It was always so. In earlier times their employer supplied the beer, etc., in addition to meals.

On 27th September, 1761, Richard Hayes, a yeoman farmer at Owletts, Cobham, Kent, already referred to, wrote in his farm diary: 'My hop dryer has his victuals and drinks no small beer. One quart of mild at evening meal and at night. Takes a quart bottle of beer out with him every night and is allowed a quart bottle of brandy to refresh himself during drying.' It is not unreasonable to suppose all this 'refreshment' would make the dryer, in the circumstances, have a problem with staying awake or sober enough to care for the hops! No doubt these men could 'hold their beer', but an intoxicated, careless dryer could wreak all sorts of havoc in an oasthouse, allowing hops to dry too much, so they 'shattered' - broke to pieces when touched, or, even worse, too much heat so the hops and drying floor, even the entire oasthouse, caught alight.

Hayes, still writing in his farm diary eleven years later, 13th September, 1772, stated : 'I went down to my oasthouse at about 4 this morning in thick fog. I heard my hop dryer

William Mace singing very melodious several psalm tunes.' Conscience pricking Mr Mace perhaps in the morning after, to stay, from now on, on the path of sobriety? Or just making merry in his work?

Hayes also recorded some costs for the task: 'For drying, a weekly wage to the dryer of from 15 shillings to 1 pound (a good wage in those days, A.M.). For bagging the dried hops 6 pence per bag.'

Experience also taught dryers the best method to cool hops. The usual method was to heap the dried hops in a pile each side of the hop press. A second method was to heap them in long, separate rows across the cooling floor, another was to spread them thinly over the cooling floor. The long-handled, wood-tined rakes were used, raking the hops to the cooling floor if the drying floor and cooling floor were close enough and a lifter cloth was not in use.

The dryer stuck to his own preferred method, even if he moved to another hop grower's oasthouse to work. A change in the method of cooling could affect a dryer's judgement as to when the hops were sufficiently cool. It also had to be kept in mind the type of weather at this time as it affected the hops on the cooling floor. If it was raining, foggy or drizzling for a considerable length of time, even if windows of the storage were kept shut, hops could absorb an unwanted amount of moisture. If the weather conditions continued, and remembering more green hops were due at the oasthouse kiln from the gardens, the dryer had to decide whether to move the hops from the cooling floor into pockets in less time than was usually required. Paradoxically, if during cooling time there had not been a sufficiently moist atmosphere the hops might not be of the required quality. It was a case of knowing the critical point to make such a decision. So the dryer's skill was all-important, success or failure resting on this one man, more so than on what type of oasthouse where the drying is taking place or the actual method of heating being used to achieve it.

Curiously, though they had been exposed to such heat, draughts and fumes, it was reputed these all beneficially 'hardened' the dryers and hands in one respect of their health because they were said rarely to catch a cold or have other respiratory problems when working or later in life.

Nor have I learned of any oasthouses in Kent and Sussex being haunted. Farms, cottages, other rural buildings, yes, oasthouses, no. This, to me, is surprising. I assumed the dryers who spent so many years of their mortal life in oasthouses could not have stayed away in the afterlife, but would want to see how the successors to their job were achieving the tasks....

A brick oasthouse, 1910, with six square kilns. Note the lucarne with its hoist and rope. The vanes on the cowls have been 'lost' against the sky. Site unknown - author would appreciate its identification. Photo: Author's collection.

The Fuels and how they were used

During the 16th century in the oasts Reynolde Scot proposed the fuel used was baulks of timber readily obtained in Kent's woodland. The snag to its use was it could create 'fumes and noxious smoake' that had to pass through the layer of hops on the drying floor above the fire before they could escape through holes made in the oast's walls, gaps in between the oast roof tiles and out through a vent in the roof, too. The 'fumes and smoake' affected the quality and flavour of the hops. Wood was replaced by virtually smokeless charcoal also available from Kent's woodlands. It was made from cordwood and timber of no use for other purposes, remaining an important fuel for hop drying for several centuries. This was despite enormous quantities needed for the task. As much as a hundred sacks of charcoal were required to dry a ton of hops in one case. Although other fuels were later available charcoal burners still travelled Kent's hop-growing districts and visited hop farms with woodland on them. For a fee they created charcoal from the hop farm's own source of timber to be used in the farm's oasthouse. The practice seems to have died out just prior to the Second World War, perhaps because by then farms could buy bagged charcoal direct from the charcoal-producing companies.

The Kentish poet, Christopher Smart (1722-1771) in his The Hop Garden refers firstly to hop growing and picking practices he knew in the county, then continues.....

'......... next succeeds
The important care of curing - quit the field,
And at the kiln the instructive muse attend,
On your hair cloth, eight inches deep, no more,
Let the green hops lie lightly; next expand
The smoothest surface with a toothy rake.
Thus far is just above, but more it boots
That charcoal flame burn equally below;
The charcoal flames, from thy corded wood
Or antiquated poles, with wondrous skill
The sable priests of Vulcan shall prepare.'

Smart refers to the task of drying hops as 'curing' them.

In the 1830s another fuel for the purpose was introduced, the hard, slow-burning, fume free, near-smokeless coal, anthracite. It came from Wales, transported to Kent and Sussex on collier ships using the counties' rivers and creeks, or by road from their seaports. The last coal-burning oasthouse in England was Little Halden Farm, Rolvenden, Kent, which ceased to grow hops in 2004.

Anthracite tended to be expensive, whereas coke, the next fuel introduced, was much cheaper. The coke was collected by farm wagon if the oasthouse was not too far away from the nearest coke source, a town's gasworks, in the 19th and early 20th century. It was cheap due to the gasworks being glad almost to give it away to get rid of it as a waste product from producing gas.

The types of kiln fires and other means of hop drying are a story in themselves. Briefly, the kiln open fires burning charcoal and anthracite on their horizontal iron bars two feet or so above the floor, comprised a rectangular brick fireplace hearth. Some of them had a spark plate, a metal sheet suspended from beneath the drying floor above the fire, the intention being to shield the hops on this floor from sparks arising from the fire, also to act as a baffle to spread the heat across the entire width of the floor underside above. Later examples of kiln fires to burn anthracite or coke had a 'roof' built of bricks, sometimes covered with cement, the wall's upper sides and back having brickwork in a 'honeycomb' style where, for several rows, every other brick was omitted to create gaps through which heat escaped.

Another 'innovation' was the multiple fire layout where there were several brick fireplace hearths with fire bars for open fires, built both sides of a narrow passage between them, the latter also built of bricks, the passage allowing access to stoke the fires. Near each fireplace hearth was a shuttered opening in the passage wall by means of which part opening, opening wider or shutting the draught to the fireplaces could be regulated. By use of these shuttered openings, and the quantity of fuel being put into the fireplaces being controlled, it was possible to regulate the heat rising to the hops on the drying floor above. A wood door by which the kiln was entered from outside sometimes also had louvres in it that could be opened or closed so as to help control the heat in the kiln; the door could be left open, too.

In the 18th century, to try and achieve even drying of a greater depth of hops on the drying floor than formerly, several arrangement plans were introduced for four fires in a central position on the ground floor of the square kilns, there being a passage that allowed each fire to be stoked separately as needed. Over the fires was a flue, the plenum chamber as it was called, being in the form of an inverted pyramid widening upwards to where it joined the underside of the drying floor. About 1780 the plaster and lath flue was replaced by an entirely brick flue that followed the previous design, but also widening as it left the fire and met the drying floor. In the later roundel kilns the same method was used, with three centrally placed fires, around them being a low circular wall. Instead of an inverted pyramid widening upwards to the drying floor, due to the kiln being round, it was an inverted cone-shaped plenum chamber.

As early as 1739 a Samuel Trowel referred to an 'iron furnace' with a 'closed grate' and a 'vent', which supplied heat required but avoided hops being affected by fumes and smoke. This would have foreseen the introduction of closed stoves burning coke, where heat was enabled to dry hops but fumes and smoke were kept separate and emitted through a 'vent' or flue. The previously mentioned John Read prepared a design for a roundel oasthouse with an enclosed fire that had a circular pipe which conveyed the heat around the roundel upwards to the drying floor so the hops were evenly dried, but the pipe exited the roundel where it joined the roof so contaminating fumes were carried away from the hops and emitted to the open air. One stove example was known as a 'cockle' stove, so-named supposedly because its dome-like upper part looked like overlapping cockle shells. Cylindrical, made of cast iron, it was closed by an iron door on one side through which fuel was fed. Iron pipes, one each side, rose from its upper part to a flue in an opposite wall, the flue having an external brick chimney for fumes and smoke emission. Because of this invention cheap, but smoke-producing, 'sea coal' could be used in this stove. The cast iron pipes of the 'cockle stove' exuded tremendous heat around it to dry the hops above.

Industry saw a demand from oasthouse owners for as perfect as possible drying system and tried to meet it with various methods. One was Shew's Patent Economic Pure-Air Heater, made by Jones & Atwood, Stourbridge, in which the fumes, via numerous pipes below the drying floor, eventually escaped out of a flue pipe sited just below the cowl. Drake & Fletcher, Maidstone, introduced a complicated 'Hop Drying Plant', with pipes zig-zagging upwards. Another 'innovation' was a 'Steam Hop-Drying Plant' by Arnold & Sons, East Peckham, incorporating a steam engine, fan and steam pipes, heated air being pushed under the drying floor above. The Sirocco System by Davidson & Co., Belfast, used a fan to blow heated air into the kiln and up to the hops, the coal and wood-burning

A Maidstone-based fire engine attending an incident at a four-roundels oasthouse in the 1950s. One cowl is missing. The oast appears to be one where a fan or fans forced hot air into the kilns, the heater plant with chimney to the exterior being housed in the adjoining shed. The kiln roofs are covered with cement rendering. Photo: Kent Fire and Rescue Service Museum, Tovil, Maidstone.

heater unit, its chimney and fan being outside the kiln in an adjoining shed.

With the temperature being produced it is not surprising destructive fires were a hazard in oasthouses. In 1942 hops on the drying floor of a kiln in the eight-kiln 1884 Crowhurst Farm oasthouse, East Peckham, caught alight damaging the roof. In 1928 the original oasthouse on Clockhouse Farm, Hunton, was gutted by fire, as was Stilstead oasthouse, East Peckham, in 1983. So, too, was Court Lodge Farm Oast, East Farleigh, a roof fire causing its destruction in 1955. Instead of the fire in the kiln being the cause sometimes an electrical fault was responsible. Not all of the destroying fires were in traditional oasthouses. In 1982 a modern steel-framed, oil-burning oasthouse, with asbestos sheet cladding, was destroyed by fire at East Farleigh.

It is no mere coincidence some of the bigger oasthouses, if possible, were in the proximity of a farm pond or other source of water, and a road for easier access for the fire engine.

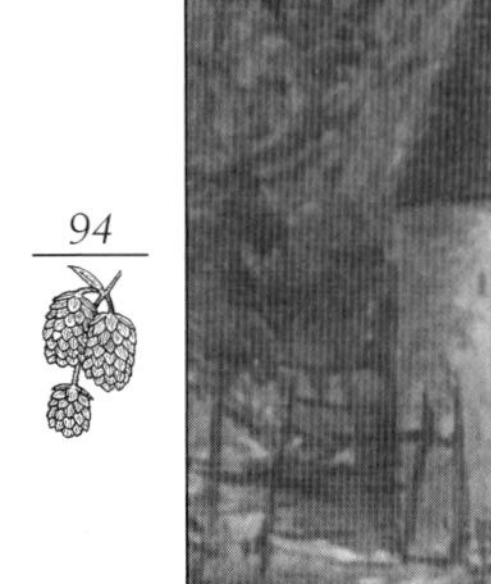

A watercolour 'Carting the hops to the London market' by C. Essinghigh Corke, 1906. They are Kent hops, the farmer's name on the pockets is Bligh, Sevenoaks. Photo: Author's collection.

More Drying 'Innovations'

In the early 20th century the need was to dry hops quicker in oasthouses between arrival as green hops and despatched dried in pockets. Also to dry a greater depth on the drying floor. Following experiments with them that had been successful in discovering the amount of forced draught needed to push more air through the deeper hop layer, six-bladed fans were introduced.

William Coles Finch, a Kent author, in 1929 commented: 'For drying the hops there is the modern introduction of electric fans to increase the draught in the kilns and so expedite the operation. In this way a given weight of hops can be dried in less time...'

In one version the fan was sited on the outer wall of the kiln at ground level and powerfully blew the heated air into the kiln and up to the underside of the drying floor and through the hops. In another version the fan was fitted into a wooden structure on the kiln roof and pulled up the air from below the drying floor and through the hops.

These fans were originally powered by using a belt driven by a steam traction engine or, later, a tractor, then, in some cases, by a Lister petrol engine and dynamo followed by diesel oil engines with a dynamo. However, when electricity reached the farms the oasthouse fans were adapted to use it. A converted-to-electricity oasthouse was indicated by the no-longer required cowls being replaced with louvred ventillators. When new oasthouses were built to use fans cowls were omitted, replaced by these louvres. Louvres on or in the roof meant the oasthouse was no longer as picturesque as it was with cowls and some would say louvred oasthouses are ugly.

Then, as anthracite had largely replaced charcoal, so cheaper oil, easier to control as a fuel, replaced anthracite, oil first being used in 1933. The early oil-burning plant was rather primitive. Usually fitted in the kiln's former coal fire hearth entrance it comprised a metal frame in which was a 'tunnel' made of firebricks. At one end was the nozzle of an oil burner compelling the hot combustion gases along the firebrick 'tunnel', the latter absorbing heat which then moved up through the hops. A later type oil-burning plant comprised a big cylindrical metal case that was also lined with firebricks. Sited in the storage, not the kiln, it had a fan at one end which also compelled the hot gases but now through metal ducts, not the kiln, to dry the hops. The oil did not contain impurities so the hops were not tainted by gases. Although oasthouse owners up to the early 1960s in Kent and Sussex continued to maintain and use their oasthouses of earlier years to dry hops changing circumstances made their obsolescence inevitable. Rapidly, virtually all oasthouses being used had sophisticated oil-fired heating complete with the thunderous roar of the oil burners; the economics of that time made this unavoidable.

In place of the human hop pickers large, industrial-type, shedlike buildings were erected to house the used-in-autumn-only hop-picking machines, idle for ten months or so in a year. Somewhere on the hop farm, too, another similar building or buildings to replace the oasthouse, a new type of kiln, was also erected to house the hop drier machinery and auxiliary services. Thus the appearance of hop farms changed within a few years, from rustic, vari-sized, brick, tile and timber oasthouses to a complex of factory-like structures. These new hop drying kilns, continuous driers, can dry a depth of some 4 feet (1.22m) of hops at one time.

Another 'advance' is that now the dried hops can be sold to brewers turned into pellets and freeze-dried, which not only saves space, as a 75 kg pocket of dried hops reduces to two 25 kg boxes, but also if vacuum-packed and put into cold storage they will stay in good condition for several years until required for use in brewing.

POCKETS OF DREAMS

Dried are our dreams, like the hops from the oasthouse
Where the vanes on the cowls lie unmoved by the breeze.
No stained pickers' hands strip the bines with thumb and finger,
No redolent fragrance, their nostrils to tease.

How precious the memories, our Kent oasts uncover,
Their mossed tiles enhancing the shadows we see
And faint on the hearing come horses and wagons
When the surplus white cowls were still swinging free.

Such fun it would be to live in an oasthouse
Reflecting on life within its round wall:
Would that scent from the hops and the past echo softly
From the seasons of picking which the oast may recall.

Push open the door and let in the sunshine;
See the beams gild the dust specks that dance on the air;
Touch and feel touched by the oast and its tokens,
Then share with its white horse+ this moment in prayer.

Warwick W. Forrester (A Man of Kent) 2004

+ A white horse, the county badge, was often fitted to cowl vanes on Kent oasthouses.

Pockets and Pokes

A pocket was, and is, a large sack, 6 feet (1.8m), up to 7 feet (2.1m) long, or high if standing upright, weighing about 168 lbs (75kg) when filled with newly pressed hops, for transporting to hop factor or brewer by cart, wagon or, later, motor lorry. It was a familiar sight met with in autumn on the roads and lanes in hop-growing areas of Kent and Sussex: horse-drawn wagons and carts, or lorries, loaded with what seemed an incredible number of hop pockets. From Faversham Creek the hop pockets also went by sailing barges upriver to London.

In the 19th century Kent hop growers faced fierce competition from the Farnham, Surrey, growers, the latter usually commanding a higher price for their hops. However, if the Farnham growers had a bad growing season and quantity and quality were down the news was received with joy in Kent and Sussex. It meant the Kent and Sussex growers could make up the shortfall by pocketing their lesser quality hops for sale to the London hop factors and get a higher price for them the year they were grown than they would if the Farnham growers had had a good season.

William Cobbett in his Rural Rides described a visit to hop growers at Chilworth, Surrey,

An empty hop pocket hanging from a beam in Beech Court Gardens Farming Museum, Challock. On the left is draped an empty poke.

in 1822, and the price paid for their hops to indicate the Surrey growers were, at times, almost beggared by the remuneration for their efforts: 'The crop of hops has been very fine here, as well as everywhere else. The crop not only large, but good in quality. They expect to get six pounds a hundred for them at Weyhill Fair. That is one more than I think they will get. The best Sussex hops were selling in the Borough of Southwark at three pounds a hundred a few days before I left London. The Farnham hops may bring double that price, but that, I think, is as much as they will and this is ruin to the hop planter. The tax, with its attendant inconveniencies, amounts to a pound a hundred; the picking, drying and bagging to 50 shillings. The carrying to market not less than 5 shillings. Here is the sum of £3.10 shillings of the money. Supposing the crop to be half a ton to the acre, the bare tillage will be 10 shillings. The poles for an acre cannot cost less than £2 a year; that is another 4 shillings to each hundred of hops. This brings the outgoings to 82 shillings. Then comes the manure, then comes the poor-rate and road-rates and county rates and if these leave one single farthing for rent I think it strange.'

If the Farnham growers did have a good growing season the Kent growers only pocketed their best quality, brightest hops. The reason was their lesser quality, dull hops probably would not sell in competition with the Farnham hops. The Kent growers kept these lesser hops back, stored in 'bags' in an oasthouse until the following year, when the Kent growers hoped the Farnham growers would have a bad season and the shortage in Surrey ensured the price paid by the factors and brewers was increased even for the Kent growers' poorer quality of hops.

It was to stop this sharp practice the marking of pockets and 'bags' was introduced and made compulsory by law. In 1774 an Act of Parliament decreed pockets of dried hops must bear details of the grower's name, farm or place name, where grown and, importantly, the year. This was intended to prevent the described fraud. It was not unknown, too, for a deceitful grower with a glut of hops and likelihood of a low price for them, deciding to retain his lesser quality hops so in the following season, should it be a poor one for the hop yield, he could mix his previous season's dried hops with the new season's dried hops to increase overall quantity. The hop samplers at the hop factors, however, were usually wise to this and could quickly tell if the pockets contained 'doctored' hops.

The terms of this 1774 Act were supplemented in 1866 by the Hop (Prevention of Fraud) Act whereby the grower again had to stencil his name, parish, county and year the hops were grown and dried, but now in prominent capital letters at least three inches high. Some growers went beyond what was officially required and included their own publicity symbols, such as medallions for national awards the grower had won. The name of the hop variety in the pocket was also sometimes stated.

The early means of marking was by using a block of wood, often hornbeam or box, with the required lettering cut on it, which was stamped on the pockets. The later stencils were sometimes made of copper but the majority of zinc as it was slow to rust or deteriorate. These stencils had the first three figures of each year, i.e. 187 or 192 as examples, the last figure being added separately when the hops were pocketed. In this way the stencils could be used for the ten years. The last figure in some years can be seen to be slightly thinner or smaller than the others. The commercial makers or suppliers of pockets today relieve the growers of this task by printing the details, via a rotary drum, on to the pocket material during manufacture. Pockets were formerly made from closely woven sacking material, usually jute; now from polypropylene.

In the 18th century it was customary for the higher quality dried hops to be put into pockets made of fine quality 'canvas', whereas those of poorer quality were put into 'bags', made of a heavy, coarse hessian, larger than pockets, holding 2 cwts. (101.6 kg) of hops.

Hop pockets, also pokes, in the late 19th century, were handmade during the prior summer by one or more of the farm's hands, usually in their spare time. A length was cut from a bolt of the sacking material after being measured to the required size, then folded and sides sewn very tightly together. The bottom or closed end was tied in such a way it formed two 'ears' each about a hand's length, used to help grasp the pocket when full.

Pockets were normally only used once for their purpose. In the 1939-45 War, however, the shortage of jute to make new pockets meant previously used pockets had to be used

A load of pockets of pressed hops, Caring Farm, Leeds, Kent, 1906. The 'ears' of the pockets visible at both ends. One of the men, top, is holding a pocket hook to help with manhandling the heavy pockets.
Photo: Author's collection.

a second time. Secondhand pockets were even sent to Kent and East Sussex growers from hop-growing areas of Worcestershire and Herefordshire. On some occasions the Herefordshire pockets were returned to their source because the presses used in that area were different to those used in Kent, so the pockets were unsuitable. Despite this some of the Kent oasthouse hands managed to adjust the neck of the Herefordshire pockets so Kent oasthouses were able to use them. These secondhand pockets from the two counties were turned inside out so the original growers' names and other details were within the pocket. After being filled in Kent oasthouses the pockets were restencilled with the Kent hop-growers' details.

A poke is a large sack-type bag made of a loosely woven material holding up to 12 bushels of green hops. The open weave of the material was intended to help stop the hops in it from sweating and deteriorating. The hops, after picking and being 'measured' out were tipped into pokes prior to transporting to the oasthouse. Another name for it was greenbag or greensack, the sack being brown and hops in it green! They are still used to convey hops from automatic hop-picking machines to the hop-drying installation.

The old saying 'To buy a pig in a poke', meaning to purchase something without seeing it, a blind sale, was reputed to have originated from the criminal practice of putting a cat in a poke or sack, with the end tied, to sell as a young pig to a gullible person, frequently at markets and fairs. Should the poke or sack be opened by the gullible person, however, the 'cat was let out of the bag', all being revealed.

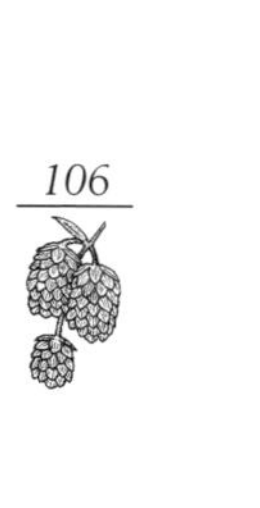

The shovel-like scuppet used to move hops on the cooling floor to the press.

Pocketing or Packeting the hops

When the hops were considered to be cool they were ready to be put into pockets. It was vital to pocket the hops by compressing them firmly in the pockets as soon as possible after cooling when their moisture content had been stabilised and evenly distributed. The compressing excluded the air and retained as much as possible of the 'resin'. Then they also kept the required quality, not deteriorating through becoming extra dry or taking in more unrequired moisture. If they were pressed before being cool enough the hops suffered spoiling known as mudging, (bruising).

An early pressing practice until the mid-to-later 19th century was treading, to tread down the hops when filling the pockets. A strong wood curb or frame with a central round hole was fitted into the cooling floor. This treading hole was, and had to be, the exact size of the mouth of the pocket. The pocket was suspended through this hole, the weight of the hops put into the pocket being supported by an iron hoop positioned under the pocket and resting on the floor. Alternatively, and more commonly, a long leather belt, suspended from hooks on the beams, passed under the bottom of the pocket and supported it.

First using a scuppet, some of the cooled hops were scuppeted, towards the round hole in the floor and then into the pocket's open mouth. A scuppet or scuppit was like a large shovel. It comprised a wooden frame, open-ended at the front, with a canvas or hessian backing, sometimes being made by the village carpenter in the past. Held by a short, digging-fork type wood handle moving the hops with it not surprisingly was known as scuppeting.

When the hops scuppeted into the pocket had settled to a depth of several inches one of the oasthouse hands, by using a short ladder, climbed down into the pocket and out of sight. Now, with his feet in thick-soled shoes or boots, the hand commenced to tread the hops down hard, in the same way as grapes were trodden for wine. When thought to be tightly compacted enough some more hops were scuppeted into the pocket. It was a thankless task few wanted to do, except those doing the scuppeting, who got some artful pleasure at pushing hops on to the man in the pocket, who was called the bagster. The bagster sometimes wisely wore a wide-brimmed hat to avoid some of the hops' deluge landing on his head. Round and round he went in the pocket below the cooling room floor level, more being added, treading these down and so on until he gradually rose higher and higher in the pocket. Appearing head, and then shoulders, then trunk at floor level, until finally he could climb out, the ladder if used having earlier been lifted out of the pocket by one of the scuppeting hands. From a roof beam above the open pocket and bagster was suspended a balance scale that was now used to weigh and learn the weight of the tightly packed pocket.

In his The Hop Farmer in 1838 E. J. Lance wrote: '....this process of treading is a tedious and unpleasant work for the men...and occasions great thirst by the quantity of dust which arises, the treader being as yellow all over as a sovereign and the yellow dust is very choking.'

The invention in the 1850s of the first mechanical hop press to take over this unpleasant task must have been a welcome boon to the oasthouse hands. It is uncertain who did solely invent the hop press, but one man with a claim is a Mr Ellis, a hop farmer at Barming near Maidstone, who had a very large acreage of hop gardens in the area in 1850, about double what other hop farmers had and thus a lot of hops to be dried and pressed.

The mechanical hop press comprises a heavy wood or cast-iron frame bolted on the floor, centrally positioned, the circular ram was wound up or down as required by turning the press' large, hand-operated wheel. This press has a rack-and-pinion principle, where the toothed wheel engages with a toothed rail, the rack. It was either a 'side-winder' or a 'front-winder', meaning if a 'side-winder' the handle and large wheel were on the side of the frame; if a 'front-winder' the large wheel and its handle were positioned on the front of the press' frame.

Beneath the ram was the round hole in the cooling floor and, as with the treading method, through the hole was suspended the pocket and its open mouth. To keep the latter open and in position the pocket mouth was fitted over an iron hoop that itself fitted

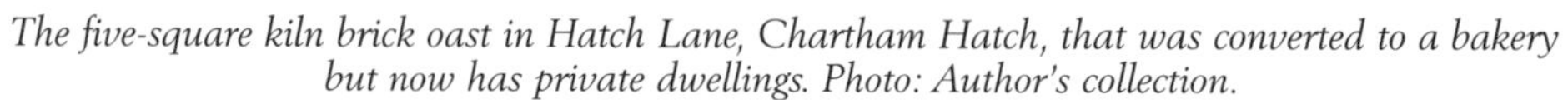

The five-square kiln brick oast in Hatch Lane, Chartham Hatch, that was converted to a bakery but now has private dwellings. Photo: Author's collection.

securely into a circular recess in the wood curb on the wooden floor. The weight of the pocket was similarly taken by a strong leather or webbing sling under the bottom of the pocket, this sling being attached to the underside of the beams of the floor above it, or by chains passing through the floor and attached to the press itself. As the hand wound the handle so the heavy iron ram descended into the open mouth of the pocket and upon the hops scuppeted into it, pressing them down as firm as it was possible to do. After this first pressing down some more hops were scuppeted into the open pocket. This process was repeated until the pocket, tight as a drum, was considered full and the approximate required weight, 1½ cwt.

It was then weighed. One method of doing this was first to put an iron bar through some iron loops on the wood curb that has the iron hoop supporting the open mouth of the pocket. On the underside of the iron ram, and to the iron bar, a spring weighing balance was attached by a hook. The ram was now wound up, raising the balance, the iron bar and iron hoop, and the wood curb. As these rose so the pocket was also suspended temporarily under the ram, free of the leather or webbing sling, the pocket's weight being noted from the spring balance scale. The pocket is lowered again onto the support of the leather or webbing sling and the balance and iron bar are removed, followed by the iron hoop supporting the mouth of the pocket. Now the open mouth of the pocket is sewn together to close it by one of the hands using strong twine and a special long, curving needle, this task being known as coping. It was done in such a way to form two 'ears' at the previously open end, one each side, these 'ears', with the two at the other closed end, helping in manhandling the filled pocket. The pocket's supporting sling was next released and the pocket was lowered on to the oasthouse's ground floor. Here it was rolled or moved on a special, flat-bottomed, two-wheeled barrow, to the storage area either in the oasthouse or a nearby building after the hop grower's details had been stencilled on the pocket. Also, to make it easier to manhandle the heavy pockets, the hands could use an iron pocket tool, a small hand-wide handle with curving hooks. The handle was grasped with the hooks downward and used like a claw on the pocket to move it.

If the hops were not being used by the brewers or sent to hop factors in the near future the pockets were stored upside down with the sewn-together open end and large 'ears' on the floor. The weight of the hops in the upper part of the pocket on those right at the bottom over time could damage the latter, so if the pocket was upside down it was simple, prior to eventual despatch, to re-open the sewn end, remove the damaged hops and replace them, then re-sew the open end.

Among the first wood-framed, iron rack and pinion hop presses were those made by the ironfounders, Pierson, at Hurst Green, Sussex, and Garretts of Maidstone, Kent, but a large number were also made by William Weeks & Son, at their Waterside Works, Maidstone. Wye College Agricultural Museum and Maidstone Museum have examples. Hop presses entirely of cast iron were later made by Weeks & Son, Maidstone, the Weald of Kent Engineering Co., Horsmonden, Kent, and Drake & Fletcher, Maidstone. Kent

Engineering and Foundry Ltd., Maidstone, and Drake & Fletcher, Maidstone, introduced automation to the pressing procedure in the 1940s using an electric motor linked to the press' 'side-winder' wheel to drive down and reverse the ram.

Hand-operated mechanical presses survive in annual use but only for pressing hops in hop history museum demonstrations, the majority of presses now in commercial use being power-driven. Another change was replacement of using hop pockets by the hydraulic hop baler but still with a ram method. Its iron frame, 18 inches (450mm) by 48 inches (1.22m), compressed rectangular bales of hops some 18 inches (450mm) deep and weighing about 200 lbs. Sewn into a cloth sheet the grower's name and the other required details were then stencilled on the bale cloth exterior after it was weighed. One maker of bale presses was Marsh Engineering, Ivychurch, Kent.

When in a former oasthouse it is sometimes possible to determine where the hole in the floor for pockets was sited. There may remain a square wood frame in the upper floor joists and best seen from underneath. If the hole 'belonged' to a mechanical press it was some distance from the oasthouse's outer wall to allow access around the press, but especially to be able to wind the handle. If the hole was close to a wall it was more likely to have been involved in the method of manually 'treading' the hops.

Three of the cowls on the five-square kilns oasthouse in Hatch Lane, Chartham Hatch. The spike-ended vanes can clearly be seen to be supported by metal rods. Note cowls' caps, too. Photo: Author's collection.

The Excise Man Cometh

An old-looking iron hook or staple may be seen on a beam in the ground floor of old oasts - a seeming mystery of what they were used for. Probably from whichever is thereon was suspended the Exciseman's official scales.

In the 18th and early 19th centuries, even if the hops were pocketed ready to despatch to the customer brewers or the hop factors they had to stay in the oasthouse's storage to await the annual visit of the Exciseman to the hop farm. In 1711 a duty was imposed on hops, this being 1 penny per poundweight on English hops and 3 pence per poundweight on imported hops. Each year every hop grower on or prior to 1st September had to send details to the Exciseman of his hop acreage, the number and sites of his oasthouses, where the hops were being bagged or pocketed, also where dried hops were being stored prior to sale. They certainly tried to ensure the hop grower did not get away with anything. No hops were allowed to be taken from oasthouses, their storage or other buildings used as store-places until every pocket or bag had been weighed in the Exciseman's presence for assessment of excise duty and marked by him or a Revenue Officer. They noted all the details of pockets or bags totals, their weights, year grown, where and grower's name.

The excise duty on hops raised considerable revenue for the Government Exchequer in good years but varied in the bad years while it was imposed, Cobbett being one who commented on it. Varying from 1 penny to 2½ pence a poundweight this variance was partly due to the abundance or otherwise of hops per acre each growing season. The duty was repealed in 1862.

The Final Rites

Another hop growing season has come and gone. The oasthouse's reason for existing is almost over once more. Some of the hop harvest may stay in pockets in storage until needed. The sampling, grading and selling is the concern of other people elsewhere. The farmer grower, dryer, hands and farm labourers have again done their best.

The task was then to close down the oasthouse. The kiln fires are now cold. The kiln draught vents shut. The ash in the kilns has been raked out using long-handled metal fire-iron rakes which will hang by hook or nail on a kiln wall. The clinkers that accumulated on the fire grate bars when burning coal or coke have been broken off, removed using the prong on the hoe-like end of the rakes intended for this purpose and discarded outside the oasthouse. The drying and cooling floors have been broom swept clean of hop debris and dust. Empty hop pokes and pockets are stacked in a corner ready for when required. The scuppets, with brooms and forks, are companied together to lean against an inside storage wall. The hop bins into which the pickers tipped their hard-won hops, are folded flat and stacked within the storage, too, along with the measurer's basket and the pole-pullers' hop hooks. Opportunity is taken to lubricate the working parts of the now still

The former two-square kilns oasthouse owned by Wakeley Brothers, Hartlip, close to Rainham railway station. On conversion to a community centre in the 1970s the interior hop drying equipment was sent to a Sussex rural life museum. When a boy the author lived in the house extreme bottom right. Note the two shedlike lucarnes.

hop press, among a general inspection and tidying up, to leave the oasthouse interior on all floors prepared to start in the following year.

The oasthouse could now 'sleep' through the winter and springtime months, until it 're-awakened' in mid-summer, with doors and windows being opened and checks of kiln fires and the press made. Fuel arrived, unless it had been bought in winter at a cheaper price, to be heaped in a close by outhouse. The kiln's drying floor was again swept and if necessary the haircloth mat was replaced. The cooling floor was swept again and then washed down. Cobwebs were swept brushed from beams and windows. Old nests of sparrows, starlings and swallows, created in the previous year on the numerous ledges by those birds who had found an entrance through a broken window, were removed. So it was in the days before the introduction of picking hops by machine and drying them automatically in hop drier machine 'sheds'.

The dryer would finally survey the oasthouse scene and contents to be sure all was indeed ready for the season-to-be. The exception was in oasthouses where the ground floor and first floor storage was used on a mixed farm for another purpose through the winter - a store for fruit or grain, housing fruit ladders and boxes, implements and equipment used for other forms of cultivation. Sometimes the ground floor was even used for farmhorse stables or cattle housing; also dry accommodation for sheep in severe winter weather. In these oasthouses only the kiln and its fire hearth or hearths, the drying and cooling floors 'slept away' the winter months. That is how it was, year in, year out.

For some of the oasthouses, however, there came a time when the previous hop-drying season was the oasthouse's last season. The human hop pickers and hop harvest did not return. These oasthouses were no longer needed due to various circumstances. They were obsolete, surplus to requirements. There are oasthouses in existence unused, forlorn in their being unwanted and in decline. Ironically some stand near to the 'industrial factory shed' that replaced them. For many others, thankfully, there has been an 'awakening', but of a different kind. Farmers and brewers' owners sold off their surplus oasthouses to new owners who could see all sorts of future for them.

The upper storey of the former Wakeley Brothers oasthouse, Rainham, in 2005, taken from a footbridge over the railway line. The cowl vanes have railway engines as symbols believed added when it was converted to a community centre. Note the two lucarnes over the hoists.

New Uses For Old Oasthouses

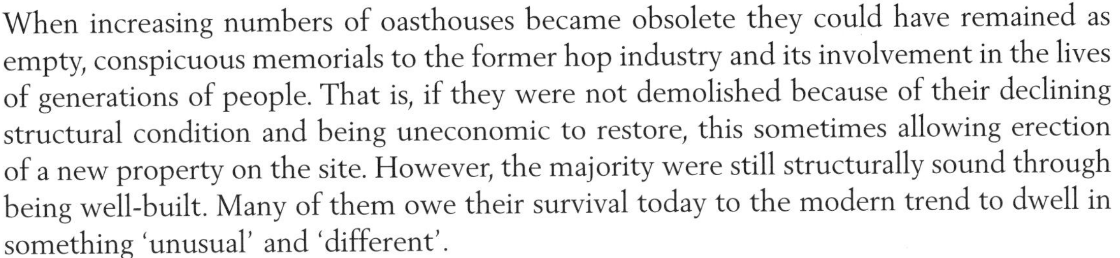

When increasing numbers of oasthouses became obsolete they could have remained as empty, conspicuous memorials to the former hop industry and its involvement in the lives of generations of people. That is, if they were not demolished because of their declining structural condition and being uneconomic to restore, this sometimes allowing erection of a new property on the site. However, the majority were still structurally sound through being well-built. Many of them owe their survival today to the modern trend to dwell in something 'unusual' and 'different'.

As dwellings oasthouses are normally little changed in exterior appearance. Even with the insertion of extra windows and doors they retain the physical character of what they once were. This is not due to pure chance. Planning authorities now, unlike earlier days, have to be consulted and permission obtained to make changes, even if they seem minor, in order to keep as much of the original oasthouse as possible, but bearing in mind modern needs. Roofs must remain tiled or slated and, if replacement is needed, originals or exact replicas of originals must be used. Control is also exercised over the size and style of new windows planned for an oasthouse conversion, particularly if for the roof. It is also strict

The former Millars Farm oasthouse near Meopham built in the 1820s but converted in 1903 to a dwelling with thirteen windows c.1906. Photo: Author's collection.

policy the cowl or cowls are not removed in such conversion to a dwelling and they have to be kept in working order and repaired when necessary. Also, to comply with present Building Regulations concerning oasthouses converted to dwellings they must have a damp-proof course. A few do already have a 19th century roofing slate course, but for those that do not a modern version is chemical insertion into the walls.

There have been eccentric exceptions. A very early example of converting an oasthouse to a dwelling, although at the time very much a 'one-off', is the former Millars Farm Oasthouse, near Meopham, Kent. It was built in the 1820s as a single roundel kiln oasthouse using the less common style of having knapped flint walls. Sir Philip Waterlow, eldest son of Sir Sydney Waterlow, 1st Bt., a Lord Mayor of London, who inherited the title in 1906, bought the oasthouse in 1903 and converted it to his own design. One which would be unlikely to be allowed today. This included having ten dormer and semi-dormer windows built into the roundels cone roof, thirteen windows in all. A later owner called it 'Tower Folly', though not a true folly, the exterior surviving today much as Waterlow knew it. Another resident was Daphne Oram, a BBC sound engineer who established the BBC's Radiophonic Workshop in 1957 and later set up her own composing and sound recording studio in the oasthouse. She was a pioneer in electronic music and sound recording, one of her achievements was recording the sound of the Tardis in the TV series 'Dr. Who'. After a stroke in 1994, causing her to enter a care home, her studio was burgled several times before 'Tower Folly' was sold, Oram dying in January, 2003.

The single roundel kiln oasthouse at Upper Hill Farm, Ulcombe, built of ragstone and bricks.

It may be thought a building such as an oasthouse with a roundel kiln would be an enormous challenge full of difficulties. Where these existed they have been overcome and the oasthouses made into comfortable homes.

An example is the single roundel kiln oasthouse at Upper Hill Farm, Ulcombe, near Maidstone, in the longtime ownership of the Maddocks family of farmers and at present lived in by one of them. The exact date of its original construction is uncertain, but being a roundel kiln most likely dates back to sometime in the 19th century, the roundel being ruinous was necessarily partially rebuilt during conversion in the 1970s. The roundel's ground floor, formerly the kiln fire, is a spacious living room; above it, reached by stairs, formerly the drying floor, is a roundel bedroom. The ground floor storage has a kitchen and w.c.; the cooling floor above it a bathroom and store room. The vane on the cowl has a black horse and a spade-shaped point. What makes this oasthouse particularly attractive and of interest is that it is built entirely of blocks of Kentish ragstone with a tiled roof, red bricks being used around them where extra windows were fitted. It is likely the ragstone was quarried in the area as it occurs where Kentish filberts and cobnuts were cultivated. Close by this oasthouse the farm still has an extensive, very old filbert plat (plantation).

In Hatch Lane, Chartham Hatch, near Canterbury, a former five-square kilns oasthouse was converted into a bakery in use for several years. When this closed the oasthouse-cum-bakery was converted again, to several dwellings.

The brick, tiled and weatherboarded rare octagonal kiln, right, on the bank of the Nailbourne, part of a former oasthouse, now dwellings, at Littlebourne.

Another view of the oasthouse, now a dwelling, at Upper Hill Farm, Ulcombe.

A relevant use was to convert them entirely or partly into museums with rural contents. An example is at Brook, near Ashford, Kent, where the oasthouse, formerly owned by Wye Agricultural College, now by the Wye Rural Museum Trust, houses a wide range of agricultural and 'hopping' items. The single roundel kiln oast was built in 1815, uniquely early for this type of kiln, as new kilns about this time were usually square.

The former Whitbread Hop Farm, Beltring, near Paddock Wood, is now the award-winning Hop Farm Country Park with numerous events and attractions for adults and children, including a hop festival week in September. Appropriately there is a Hop Story Museum in one of the oasthouses. In another are stabled six of the famous Whitbread Shire Horses that formerly worked on the farm and now perform displays and provide beer dray rides around the farm. And if you so desire you can get married in one of the oasthouses licensed for the purpose and also hold the reception on the Hop Farm, too.

Similar is the Heaven Farm Leisure complex, Furners Green, Danehill, Sussex. In 1835 two oasthouses were built on the farm to a Hereford oasthouse design. About 1901 one collapsed and no hops were dried on the farm after then, the surviving example having varied uses. As a wood shed, the cooling floor for deep-litter chickens, after that as a hay and straw store. In recent years the oasthouse has been part of the farm museum, but currently has planning permission for conversion to a dwelling.

At the National Trust's Sissinghurst Castle, formerly home of Victoria Sackville-West who

Heaven Farm Leisure Complex, Furners Green, Danehill, Sussex.
The former oasthouse is in the top righthand corner.
Photo: Sussex Top Attractions Ltd.

wrote about it and various aspects of 'hopping' days, the oasthouse has six 18th century square kilns and two 19th century roundel kilns, hops last being dried therein in 1967. It had a chequered history, the cooling floor at present housing a 'hopping' and local history exhibition, some of the kilns having a café and shops catering for visitors.

Those readers who would enjoy a cup of tea or coffee and cakes in a former oasthouse roundel kiln that still retains its original drying floor with visible slats above their heads, can do so. At Beech Court Gardens, near Challock, the former 19th century oasthouse, last used for its original purpose in the 1900s, was converted into tearooms in 1995. The ground floor storage is also part of the tearooms. There can be few former oasthouses in such a beautiful setting as this one among these gardens.

A 19th century oasthouse, Bough Beech Oast, between Edenbridge and Sevenoaks, has been a visitor centre for the Kent Wildlife Trust since 1981, run in partnership with Sutton and East Surrey Water, being just north of Bough Beech Reservoir. It has displays concerning the oasthouse's history, the reservoir and adjacent nature reserve's wild life. On the single roundel kiln's cowl vane is depicted a hop bin and two people involved in 'hop measuring' from it.

A number of oasthouses have been converted into farm shops. At Perry Court Farm, Canterbury Road, Boughton Aluph, the shop is in an oasthouse formerly with one roundel kiln and one square kiln, the cooling floor being in between. The roundel kiln no

A view of Perry Court Farm Oast, from the east side, 2005, now a farm shop. The base of the roundel kiln has had its cone roof replaced by one of flat, corrugated iron. The end brick wall of the former cooling floor and storage has corrugated iron cladding.

longer has its cone roof and cowl and the roof of the cowl-less square kiln has been capped, but the original low beams and walls indicate the former use.

A late Victorian malt oast, owned by Canterbury Council and now used as a store, close by Canterbury castle, has part of a Presbyterian chapel, that was against it until the 1930s, still embedded in the oast's rear wall.

For those who cannot afford to buy and live in their own former oasthouse, but would like to experience living in one for a short time, this is possible as examples in Kent and Sussex are available as holiday accommodation, either bed and breakfast or self-catering.

In Kent these include (b.and b.): Bishopsdale Oast, Biddenden; Bull Farm Oast, Cranbrook; 17th century Hallwood Farm Oast, Cranbrook; Leavers Oast, Hadlow, Tonbridge; Goldings Oast, Hunton, Maidstone; Chequers Oast, Lamberhurst; Langley Oast, Langley Park, Maidstone; Hereford Oast, Smarden; Sparks Oast Farm, Sutton Valence - (s.c.): Arundel Oast, High Halden; Penn Court Oast, Hollingbourne; Barnfield Oast, Mount Pleasant, Lamberhurst. In Sussex these include (s.c.) the 19th century Oast House, Chiddingly; (b. and b. hotel) two-roundel Playden Oast, near Rye.

Nashenden Farm Oast, Borstal, built 1877, pre-war had different annual occupants. In the 1920s and 1930s companies of Girl Guides held a camp on the farm. During inclement weather they ate and slept in the oasthouse. In 1988 it was converted into two four-bedroomed dwellings. The oasthouse is depicted in the Nashenden Valley scene, part of

The late Victorian brick malt oast adjoining Canterbury castle.
The cowl has gone from the single kiln but the cowl kerb can be seen. Photo: Author's collection.

the Women's Institute 'Domesday' Tapestry in St. Matthews church, Borstal.

A theatre in a converted two-roundel kilns oasthouse is the Tonbridge Oast Theatre, opened by Lady Nevill in 1974. In 1838 it had comprised only an oblong building, close to a large hop garden and arable land, the two roundels being added in the early 1860s. Until 1970 it was a working oasthouse, but when put on sale for £7000 the Tonbridge Theatre & Arts Club bought it after much fund-raising in various ways and then hard work to convert it at an eventual cost of £29,000, to become the thriving 112-seater theatre. In April, 1988, a major extension was opened by Prince Edward.

'The First Oasthouse Theatre in the World' is a title rightly claimed for the theatre owned by the Rainham Theatrical Society. In 1961 about one-third of the 19th century Stratford Lane oasthouse off the High Street, Rainham was offered for sale by the owner, local farmer Jack Clark, as no longer required for the remaining working oasthouse. However, Clark allowed it to be used free as a theatre for a while and later it was rented. Society members converted it to a theatre that opened in November, 1963, with a production of 'Billy Liar', as 'The World's Only Oasthouse Theatre', as it then was. Eventually the Society's founders decided in 1966 to buy the theatre part of the building from Clark for £4,800. Until the 1970s the theatre continued to share the building with the working part of the oasthouse on the other side of a dividing partition! There was, fortunately, an agreement with the hop dryer that sulphur would not be used in the hop drying until after 10 o'clock on evenings when plays were being performed, because the heady

'The First Oasthouse Theatre in the World', the Oasthouse Theatre, Rainham. Photo: Rainham Theatrical Society.

sulphur fumes, added to the soporific hops, could affect the concentration of the audience! Since then improving changes have been made to the interior, but the exterior remains basically the original oasthouse. Today it is an oasthouse with two uses. One part is the theatre; the other, larger part, the former working oasthouse eventually closed in 1988, was converted into present dwellings.

Lastly is the example of an 'oasthouse' constructed for use as... a public house. In Grove Green Road, Weavering, Maidstone, is the 'Early Bird'. It was built in 1989 by brewers Shepherd Neame, Faversham, with the exterior in the style of a typical Kentish oasthouse, complete with roundel kiln and cowl with a vane. The name of this novelty 'public house' is apt because 'Amos' Early Bird' is the name of an old, early-in-the-picking-season hop variety, bred in Kent by one Alfred Amos of Wye.

These oasthouse examples with varied uses, even though hop growing and harvesting in the old way is becoming history, mean numerous oasthouses in Kent and Sussex remain a traditional part of the landscape of these counties. Long may they do so.

The 'Early Bird' public house, Weavering, Maidstone, built in the style of an oasthouse. Photo: Shepherd Neame Ltd., Faversham.

The three-kiln oasthouse at Littlebourne, the Nailbourne flowing past on the other side. The uncommon octagonal kiln is second from right, narrower than the other two square kilns.

Modern style 'oast cowl' vents at Bluewater shopping centre, Dartford 1999.
Photo: Diana Bailey.

Acknowledgements

The author acknowledges, with his grateful thanks, those listed herewith who assisted him during the research for and writing of this book:

Valerie Armstrong, The Oast Theatre, Matfield, Tonbridge (Information and photographs).

Diana Bailey (information and photographs).

Tony Blake, Chestfield, Kent (information).

Andrew and Stephanie Buckworth, Caroline Chatfield, Sturry, Kent (sundry assistance).

Marvin Burridge, Thruxted Farm, Mystole, Kent (information).

John Butler, Heaven Farm Leisure Complex, Furner's Green, Danehill, Sussex (information).

Canterbury Public Library Local Archives Staff.

Pip Dodd, Administrator, Scotney Castle garden and estate, National Trust, Lamberhurst, Kent (information).

The Hop Farm Country Park, Paddock Wood, Kent (information and loan of photograph).

Warwick Forrester, South Marston, Wiltshire (for permission to use his poem Pockets of Dreams).

Paul Gardiner, Chart Court Oast, Little Chart, Kent (CD's, photographs and information).

Brenda Pearson and M. Harbour, Rainham Theatrical Society (information and photograph).

John Meakins, Museum Curator, and the Kent Fire & Rescue Service Museum, Tovil, Maidstone (information and loan of photograph).

Chris Nicholas, Hoad's Farm, Sandhurst, Kent (information).

Vic Nutting, Rainham, Kent (sundry assistance).

Michael Scanlon, Ref. Librarian, Defra Information Centre, London (information).

T. W. Smith, Grower Liaison Manager, Botanix (formerly the Hop Marketing Board, Hop Pocket Lane, Paddock Wood, Kent (information).

Graham Snelling, Curator, National Horseracing Museum, Newmarket, Suffolk (information).

Especial thanks to Mabel Maddocks, Upper Hill Farm Oasthouse, Ulcombe, and to the other owners and residents of oasthouses who generously invited the author to see their properties and the present day use. Thanks also to Ron Maddocks for allowing the photographing of his Ulcombe oasthouse.

~ ~ ~ ~ ~

The author also puts on record his thanks to his grand-daughter, Frances Buckworth, for transferring her grandfather's manuscript on to disk for publication.

PICTURE CREDITS

The majority of the photographs are by the author. Those which are not are individually credited. The source of several photographs collected by the author was not stated on them and efforts to trace the photographer/publisher were unsuccessful. The author apologises for any unintended infringement of copyright and if informed of these details will credit source/owner if reprinted.

Bibliography

Arnold, Ralph. A Yeoman of Kent. Constable, 1949

Brunskill, R. W.. Traditional Farm Buildings of Britain. Gollancz, 1982

Church, Richard. Kent. Robert Hale, Ltd., 1949

Cronk, Anthony. Oasts in Kent and Sussex, Pt 1. Archaeologia Cantiana, Vol. XCIV, 1978

Cronk, Anthony. Oasts in Kent and Sussex, Pt II. Archaeologia Cantiana, Vol. XCV, 1979

Finch, William Coles. Life in Rural England. Daniel & Co., 1929

Harvey, Nigel. A History of Farm Buildings in England & Wales. David & Charles, 1970

Hefferman, Hilary. Voices of Kent's Hop Gardens. Tempus, 2000

Lawrence, Margaret. The Encircling Hop. Sawd, 1990

Marshall, William. The Rural Economy of the Southern Counties. 1798

Scot, Reynolde. A Perfite Platform of a Hoppe Garden, etc.. 1574

Stevens, Peter. Hop-picking in Faversham, the locals remember. Faversham Society, 1999

Trowell, Samuel. A New Treatise of Husbandry, Gardening and other curious matters relating to country affairs. 1739

Tusser, Thomas. Five Hundred Points of Good Husbandry. 1573

Whitlock, Ralph. A Short History of Farming in Britain. John Baker, 1965

~ ~ ~ ~ ~

For indepth study of the history, construction and equipment of oasthouses in Kent the author recommends Kentish Oasts, 16th-20th century, by Robin and Ivan Walton (Christine Swift, 1998) and for both counties, Oasthouses in Sussex and Kent, their history and development, by Gwen Jones and John Bell, Phillimore, 1992, and also for hops, hop picking and oasthouses in general in England, Hops and Hop Picking, by Richard Filmer, Shire Publications, 1982. Also useful for walkers/visitors Hops and Downs, leaflet by Dave Hughes, Tourism Plus, produced by Mid-Kent Leader with K.C.C.